Papers for P

PAPERS FOR PAY

Confessions of an Academic Forger

Jeffrey Alfred Ruth

McFarland & Company, Inc., Publishers

Jefferson, North Carolina

LIBRARY OF CONGRESS CATALOGUING-IN-PUBLICATION DATA

Ruth, Jeffrey Alfred, 1971–
    Papers for pay : confessions of an academic forger / Jeffrey Alfred Ruth.
        p.   cm.
    Includes bibliographical references and index.

    ISBN 978-0-7864-9688-4 (softcover : acid free paper) ∞
    ISBN 978-1-4766-1866-1 (ebook)

    1. Academic writing—Moral and ethical aspects.   2. Authorship—Moral and ethical aspects.   3. Internet research—Moral and ethical aspects.   4. Plagiarism.   I. Title.

    LB2369.R89 2015
    808.02'5—dc23   2014047652

BRITISH LIBRARY CATALOGUING DATA ARE AVAILABLE

Cover images iStock/Thinkstock

Printed in the United States of America

McFarland & Company, Inc., Publishers
    Box 611, Jefferson, North Carolina 28640
    www.mcfarlandpub.com

This book is dedicated to my wife Victoria. At various times during our heretofore twenty-two-year marriage, I have been a liar, a legacy, and a loser in our relationship. In addition, I feel that although she has always been my biggest fan, I should acknowledge that her disdain for Ossi Chesterton is just as strong. For that, she is certainly not to blame, and perhaps should be lauded instead! You are a blessing to me, and I love you.

To my children who have loved me and encouraged me during all of my writing days, thank you and I love you more than my words can express. Kyrin, Jordan, Evan, Brendan, and Lorien have celebrated every milestone in my career, making me feel like I have written the most wonderful things ever—every time.

I could never have gotten this far without all of you.

Acknowledgments

A book like this, in fact a journey like this one, needs support and encouragement from even the days before research commences. The list of those who have contributed to this moment is lengthy, and I will undoubtedly fail in my efforts to thank all who deserve it. Please accept my apologies in advance, and know that in my heart and mind I realize the help you have all been.

To all those who have provided the daily encouragement and interest in my writing necessary for me to believe in myself, thank you. As the project wound down, Jeff, Maria, and Roger Zerndt provided me a welcoming environment and wonderful coffee at Teeko's Coffee & Tea in Howell, Michigan. Much of the final text was typed there.

To the real academicians behind my writing development, I cannot thank you enough. Ronald Sudol, former dean of the College of Arts and Sciences at Oakland University, Rochester, Michigan, was an early mentor who accepted me into the academic realm. Professor Niels Herold, Renaissance drama and Shakespeare expert at Oakland University, somehow remains a close friend and supporter despite the fact that he has a growing awareness of my shady work in the areas of his expertise. Ossi owes you a cognac. Professors Anjili Babbar, Jacob Blumner, Tom Foster, and Annemarie Toebosch, all of whom I studied under while at the University of Michigan, Flint, honed my skills and made me feel more like a colleague than a student. Professor Babbar, in particular, continues to encourage my work, for which I extremely grateful.

The forger himself, Ossi Chesterton, would like to acknowledge the unwitting support that a certain bar and grill in Ann Arbor, Michigan, offered. The ambience provided by the college crowds collected under the big martini logo gave him a place that was all his. For all of the places that would rationally judge his activities harshly, it was never that way there. Sorry to have involved you, but thanks for the safety, comfort, and inspiration that you offered.

Finally, to the new writing group that I am privileged to be a part of, The What Box, thank you for allowing me to share this book and bounce ideas off of you. I am looking forward to all of our projects together in the future.

Table of Contents

Table of Contents

Preface

Research extrapolated from a study of recent essay writing organizations indicates that as many as 1,800,000 purchased academic papers are submitted across the United States each academic term. That accounts for nearly four million forgeries each year, not counting shorter terms like Spring and Summer. Clearly the business of academic forgery is thriving. Despite the emergence of Turnitin and other proprietary tools to detect these cheats, clever forgers—and the companies that employ them—have found numerous ways to ply their trade. The result is a lucrative enterprise, much to the chagrin of not only college professors, but high school teachers as well.

Over a period of six months in 2010, I wrote as the academic forger Ossi Chesterton, immersing myself in this subculture as an undercover staff writer with a company which I will call FraudPapers. (This is not its real name. Nor is it the first false name I have made up for the company, for between the time I wrote this and the time this book was going to press, a real company had sprung up under my original name, with a website promising more than 200 freelance writers ready to turn out essays, research papers and more.) This temporary career choice began, admittedly, as do those of typical academic forgers; i.e., I was an out-of-work university graduate who held a bachelor of arts degree in English. Even with the Writing Specialization distinction attached, this meant very little when it came to the job market. So I turned to this tawdry option. During my relatively short time with this prominent essay-writing company, I completed more than three hundred assignments for students around the globe. My previous experience as a published academician and a literary forgery student helped me quickly rise to the top rung of the company's writing staff. In this capacity, I became privy to many trade secrets through access to the company's entire order database and partnership with my personal account manager. What I found shocked me. Work had turned to intrigue. Intrigue then turned to research.

By showing the impossibility of closing all avenues of academic dishonesty, *Papers for Pay* will at once dismay, entertain and inform both the academic and popular reader through the often tongue-in-cheek stories of everyday life as a forger. These vignettes are tied into topical analysis and exposition of the key areas of academic forgery that are vital for the American culture to understand.

In this book, I describe three categories of essay writing clients:

- Career cheaters, who have no qualms about outsourcing much of their collegiate work. These clients often try several writers in a company's stable until they find a favorite; from that point this individual becomes their personal writer, at a premium cost increase.
- Honest cheats, who usually offer a variety of legitimate-sounding reasons for turning to writing assistance. Their excuses range from attempting to balance work and academics, to having to finish college as quickly as possible in order to support their family.
- Cheater networks, which tend to spring up in assignments from introductory level college courses. Sometimes these friends inadvertently implicate each other through their orders, while others specifically address the issue, imploring writers to avoid plagiarizing the group's papers. This category is most concerned with being caught and least apologetic about paying for papers.

It is my aim to fully expose for the first time this underground realm in which instructors, students, and forgers all operate, each with a different objective. Instructors pursue students, attempting to enforce integrity standards; students pursue instructors, seeking ways to get around the rules; ironically, no one pursues the forgers who create their own rules, meeting deadlines and making money.

Papers for Pay invites readers into the experience of one such forger. I cover a wide range of topics in this book in a seminar fashion, from the obvious mechanisms of forgery to the farcical requests of desperate clients. Readers will quickly understand the serious implications of this fascinating field; despite advancements in plagiarism detection, it appears that academic forgers still remain ahead of the game—their game.

Each chapter of this book will share one topic in two sections. First, the forger Ossi Chesterton will introduce the subject in a first person vignette (in *italics*) called **The Forger at Work**. This will provide context, along with a bit of humor. The next section, the **Seminar**, will delve into the topic with much more detail. It will give the facts, implications and applicability to the education world today.

The work begins with a discussion of the prevalence and general reasons for the recent trend in academic cheating of this nature, along with an introduction to the forger's daily life. Subsequent chapters present topical elements along with experiences as seen through the forger's eyes. I describe why forgery is on the rise and how typical students become aware of, and use, the various services provided via the Internet. The book also covers the difficulties of proving academic forgery, and the relative ease with which skilled forgers can produce even the most complicated papers, seemingly at a moment's notice.

The field of academic forgery is fairly under-represented in the educated reader market today. While memoirs approach this topic from a dynamic, story-driven approach, they fail to identify the culturally relevant aspects of forgery. In addition, they do not offer topical instruction or suggestions to academia regarding this form of dishonesty as a whole. On the other hand, academic approaches to the subject often weigh themselves down under the burden of inaccessible language, or remain nebulous and philosophical instead of directly attacking the problem. Neither genre truly combines specificity with entertainment.

One fine book that attempts to describe, and solve for, academic forgery is *Cheating in School: What We Know and What We Can Do* by Stephen F. Davis, Tricia Bertram Gallant, and Patrick F. Drinan (2009).[1] Its strengths are its clear approach and language, which make it an easy read. However, its treatment of cheating as merely a general academic malaise renders its information a bit too broad to be usable as a preventive measure against this sort of fraud. The present work focuses on the specific issue of academic forgery, rather than a grouping of problems found in academia. This will prove more successful in not only better identifying the problem, but also in providing truly helpful suggestions regarding how to solve for it.

Cheating in College: Why Students Do It and What Educators Can Do About It by Donald L. McCabe, Kenneth D. Butterfield, and Linda K. Treviño (2012) is a quality effort.[2] It does make the connection between cheating and college students, but chooses to focus instead on a more philosophical, less pragmatic angle. It also concentrates on the subject of academic integrity rather than the tools of cheating, which leaves the reader wanting regarding the methods of this underground work. This book further explores the various educational levels of cheating, but draws readers much farther in to the problem with its contemporary, cultural connections found only in a specific forger's story. As a result, the audience will more fully appreciate not only what is going on in their kids' schools, but also how it is happening.

A different twist on the subject can be found in *The Shadow Scholar: How I Made a Living Helping College Kids Cheat* by Dave Tomar (2013).[3] It is a story told by an academic forger, and covers the intrigues and dramas of his alternate lifestyle as professional cheat. Certainly its strength comes from the force of its storytelling, but it doesn't find a place in the more academically aimed market. *Papers for Pay* takes the power of the forger's voice and weaves it into and around a strong base of academic investigation and cultural commentary. The result is a multifaceted and objective treatment of the topic, and a much broader relevancy with educated readers.

Although I choose not to drive the book with a memoir treatment, the text reveals the challenges I faced and the satisfaction I enjoyed as I lived the life of a forger. What emerges is not only a thorough presentation of the timely subject, but a catch-me-if-you-can challenge for the academic world.

Introduction: Meet Ossi Chesterton, Academic Forger

by Jeffrey Alfred Ruth

"I could give you my name, but it simply wouldn't matter. Maybe it's Ossi, maybe it's not. The important thing is it will never appear on your paper because I am careful and I know how to play the game. I write papers for a living. Not just any papers—academic papers. Not just any academic papers—your academic papers. I am an academic forger."

Somewhere this is shocking someone more than just you, the average reader. It's not the confessional aspect but the words themselves. I left this exact passage on a young man's clipboard in Ann Arbor, Michigan, some time ago. He was sitting in front of a coffee shop at one of those metal grating sort of tables, designed to look like cast iron even though it's really not. That's sort of ironic, isn't it? The sign on the chair next to him invited passers-by to come share their stories with him. The aim of the project apparently was to see if complete strangers on the street would share their most personal, intimate stories and secrets in writing. I couldn't help myself. Maybe I was feeling cocky. Did I mention that this café is right on the campus of the prestigious University of Michigan?

So I jotted down those words and headed back onto the leafy walks of Michigan. As I enjoyed the gothic architecture and vine-covered buildings I wondered just how long it would take him to read my words. I still wonder. It was the first public confession of my forgeries.

That was over three hundred forgeries ago. I would love to be able to say that I started this project just like the "share your stories" man, that it was a noble effort to understand and expose the world of academic forgery. That's just not true, though. Like many other forgers I was an out-of-work English major, trying to find some way to support my family in a field other than retail. Or fast food. I probably shouldn't have written that. I mean no slight to burger-flippers. It is just the writer's ego talking. We all think we're so special, writers that is. Maybe that's what is so appealing about academic forgery.

I would also like to think that I eventually took on orders as research, to finally let academia in on this bane. It is true. I am coming clean. At the same time, though, it was fun. And addictive. Take the moment I decided to write this book, for instance. I was sitting at a bar, a fairly swanky national chain with a martini as its logo. I was drinking one as I wrote, and thinking about turning on my fellow forgers. At the same time, I still had three papers due to various clients the next day and to be honest with you I didn't even know what they were about. No problems, though. I was good. I'd learned to research, analyze, synthesize, and produce in usually under four hours. Three papers tomorrow would be no problem. I even had time for a refreshing after-drink walk along the lake that night. Then it would be back to the deadlines.

That was what my life looked like in 2010 when I found myself immersed in the world of academic forgery in America. I had no idea when I began that the field was as active and pervasive as I would find it to be. When I took on the job with the company I'm calling Fraud-Papers (one of nearly countless pay-for-papers outlets) I had serious doubts. I wondered if they were, indeed, "real" business opportunities. I worried that they wouldn't pay. It turns out that the business is "real" all right. When the first paycheck arrived, it was for a paltry hundred and sixty dollars or so, but I was relieved nonetheless.

During the six months of my life as Ossi Chesterton, academic forger, I wrote over three hundred papers. According to FraudPapers, there were a couple of hundred writers active during that time in their own company alone. Extrapolated, that means if I wrote fifty papers a month and the others wrote likewise, then at least 6,000 works of genuine fraud were submitted to institutions per month. The average school term is three months, so FraudPapers was responsible for over 18,000 papers each marking period that I was with them. Those are conservative figures, unfortunately. And there are many similar companies in operation today, all accessible with the click of a mouse. The implications are staggering.

Before going too much further, it should be pointed out that there is a difference between academic forgery and academic plagiarism. This will be covered in depth later in the book, but here are the definitions, briefly: forged papers are original in nature, with accurate research and writing created by the forger himself; plagiarized papers are simply copied from other sources, reputable or not. Additionally, in the forger's world there are three types of people: the instructors who pursue dishonest students, attempting to enforce integrity standards; students who pursue the instructors, seeking to get around the rules; and the forgers whom no one actually pursues, creating their own rules, meeting deadlines, and making money.

For those of you professionally involved in academia, to you students, and yes, even to you concerned parents, what follows is a firsthand exploration of academic forgery in America today; I hope it will entertain and maybe surprise you. Welcome to the forger's world.

1
Foundations for Forgery

The Forger at Work: *I never intended to be a forger. That is probably the case for most of the staff writers in the essay industry. Let's face it, when the career counselors in school come to students with potential job placement matches, "academic forger" just isn't one of the choices. But the term "college student" sure gets tossed around a lot. That tends to scare many high schoolers, and therein lies the problem for them, and the opportunity for forgers like me. Many people just aren't cut out for college, at least at first. On the other hand, there are many students who are shocked by just how easy college classes are to them. This dichotomy is the perfect foundation for forgery.*

It's not long before the various groups shake themselves out, generally within the first few weeks of beginning college. Before long, the good students keep to themselves and their work, and the not-so-good students begin to, well, not keep to themselves. They seek help.

The upstanding among them seek assistance appropriately. Study halls, tutors, and the instructors themselves receive their queries. Then there are the students with fewer moral restraints. Enter the forgers.

I can't stress enough the fact that writers for the so-called paper mills aren't necessarily bad people. This isn't just to make myself feel better about my day job. Really. I was one of those students in high school, and even earlier, who paid attention to and attempted to honor the traditional methods of the American school system. Coming from a middle- to upper-middle-class suburb in the Midwest, it would have been difficult to escape these expectations. I took pre-college courses through my secondary education experience and although I didn't excel (mostly due to immaturity and a bit of irresponsibility sprinkled in) I did well enough to get into the colleges to which I applied. That was the goal, and I got there. And no, I didn't go there to study forgery, although interestingly enough I did research literary forgery in my undergraduate capstone course. For the record, the instructor responsible for that class did not inspire my later career with FraudPapers. Honest.

So there is my background. Typical kid, traditional curricular methods. And now I'm a forger. How could this have happened to good old me? How did I become Ossi Chesterton?

Mostly because I feel that I have been lied to all along.

I've never been perfect, especially in my young adulthood, but I did toe the line pretty well. When I packed my bags for university study, I was ambitious about my plans to succeed and then become a professional writer and/or college professor. My high school counselors assured me this could happen. I still have the signature of a teacher early on who wrote in a yearbook of mine, "You should be a great writer. I'm sure I'll see you in Who's Who." *Boy, she should see me now! I bet she'd be very surprised, and unfortunately very disappointed. But then again, I'm just as disappointed. To continue where my guidance counselors left off, I was bolstered in my beliefs by my very first freshman sections of rhetoric. I excelled. Every paper I turned in was stronger than the last, and I earned straight "A" grades. Professors started inviting me to their office hours to discuss where I could go from there. They guided me and helped to hone my writing style even more. I was sent off to conferences where I presented my research papers in support of both myself and the university. I was already one of them, those elites who stand behind the lectern every class. I felt that I belonged even before graduation. Some trusted staff indicated to me that they even considered me to be like faculty as I approached my final semester. Then it all fell down.*

I have twelve awards and scholarships on my curriculum vitae. *All of them are for undergraduate work. Not a dime for graduate school. I could really use some dimes for my martini habit right about now.*

I run my own graduate school at this moment. Here I am behind the lectern. It is a well-worn wooden high top table at the window side of the bar. I love this seat. First of all, the neon glare from the martini sign over the sidewalk glints off the screen in front of me. It's a bit distracting at times when it obscures the title pages of my essays, but it feels like home to me. The sidewalk, by the way, is the other draw of this spot. Back and forth they walk, those rising young stars of the academic realm. Up and down they walk to central campus, books in hand, lattes to lips.

And Ossi's essays in their folders.

Again, welcome to my world. Sit down, listen to the swizzle stick and the key taps. Whatever you do, don't bother the students partying all around you. After all, they've got papers due in the morning.

Seminar: The stage for academic forgery is set very early on in the collegiate experience. Each institution has a course named college composition, or basic rhetoric, or a variety of other titles. These are the classes that a student must pass to proceed further along the academic ladder. Completing this prerequisite represents the ability to produce passable, quality writing in many forms, including research and composition, and is likely indicative of future academic success. In fact, many schools do not allow their freshmen to proceed to the second semester if they do not get through the first composition class with a passing grade. In truth, they are absolutely correct in this policy. Each and every major requires the ability to synthesize findings and opinions into well-written documentation. Whether for creative endeavors, or more scientific undertakings, the grasp of the written English language is a must. This is the first hurdle that college students face. As soon as the first session starts, it is apparent that there are two groups sitting in the room: those who can, and those who can't.

This is the first thing that the advanced student notices. It must be true of the professors as well, but I never asked when I was in school. I was only interested in just how it was that many college students didn't know how to write a proper essay. The fear in their eyes when the instructor started talking about the syllabus and deadlines showed itself in the shuffling of papers and chairs and the whispers of side conversations. It was clear that some of those students just weren't going to pass the first time around. And they didn't, even as many other student writers passed with top grades. By then, the lesson had been learned by both groups. The gate to higher learning was shut and barred for some by that one course. If these future mathematicians, scientists, businessmen and others were going to get to their careers, they would need some significant help. Otherwise, they would be forever mired in academia, seeking a way out. Without a degree they would never see their aims come to fruition. Fortunately for me, I didn't experience this difficulty in freshman writing.

Years later, I graduated from that same university *summa cum laude* with a degree in English, and was awarded the writing specialization distinction, no less. My dreams were coming true, as I expect everyone's were that day, too. As I walked down the aisle, out of the auditorium and on to my own future, I knew that one of two things would happen. I would either go directly to graduate school, or I would become a professional writer. I never anticipated that I would be on to Plan C before long.

These are indeed the foundational aspects for why writers become forgers. Plan A for the majority of English majors is to go to graduate school. Whether they are aspiring writers seeking a master's in Fine Arts, or are planning to be professors looking to gain their doctorate, it is the terminal degree that will lead them there. However, there are significant problems with that plan, as it turns out. To begin with, most depend upon financial aid to carry them through. During my undergraduate years, I not only had a full ride scholarship through various benefactors, but I made money as well. This was due to stipends, grants, and awards beyond that necessary for tuition and fees. For some reason still not known to me, the University forwarded this extra money to me every semester. I not only had all my expenses paid for, but I had gas and coffee money left over, which was a boon for a commuting student.

Therefore, I expected that with my academic and financial aid history this would continue into graduate school, especially since I was accepted *pro forma* into the program. That is when I found out that I would only be receiving a five hundred dollar grant which left me thousands upon thousands of dollars short. I thought there was a mistake and so I gathered my transcripts and did my "perhaps you don't remember me, the golden child" routine at the financial aid office. "Oh yes, didn't you receive your five hundred dollars yet? Is that the problem?" That certainly was the problem because they just didn't have any other money to offer. I withdrew from graduate school. So much for Plan A.

I had been working on a book during much of my last two years of baccalaureate studies so I returned to it as I began looking for a freelance writing job. As the months passed, the book began shaping up, but the employment search wasn't going so well. Staff writing positions seemed to be full, and many of them required advanced degrees anyway. There were many freelance positions advertised on various sites but they often paid less than a dollar per completed page which I found to be both insulting and impossible to live on. Once or twice I came across online comments about essay writing services but never really paid attention as they seemed both unethical and smacked of the possibility of scams. There had to be jobs out there if I was just persistent enough. During this time my family and friends started inquiring about my findings. They could not understand why I was not going to graduate school and the feeling was that I didn't want to because I thought that I was a good enough writer and wanted to see those ambitions fulfilled. They were partially right, of course. I would always choose a writing career over any other. It wasn't bravado, though, that kept me from trying for my own Ph.D., as I assured those who were asking. They weren't convinced. That is how strong the belief in traditional schooling is.

Eventually I began looking at the services. The first thing that struck me was just how many of them there were. I stopped counting at the one hundred mark. The second thing was that these companies were blatantly advertising their wares. There was nothing subtle. Each ad screamed "buy essays here." They promised quick papers, expert papers, no plagiarism papers, business papers, English papers, even English as a second language papers. The possibilities were endless. And the money? Judging from the per page prices that the companies were asking of the clients, a minimum of six dollars a page, I just knew that the writers had to be making more than the typical freelance positions I had seen and declined in my earlier job searches. This leads to the first foundation for why academic forgery exists and is so prevalent in the United States today.

Foundation One: The Myth of the English Major

I've already talked about being a writer in college. A darned good writer, I might add. This had always been my strength growing up and I fancied becoming a professional author at some point. Unfortunately for me, all of my teachers thought this was a great idea, too. This is called the myth of the English major. Our colleges are still largely based upon the classics and this encourages one to believe that the arts are still a viable way to become educated and make a living. As many bachelor of arts degree holders will tell you (and especially English majors) this certainly makes one qualified to check corporate pizza boxes for editing mistakes. The fallacy that is taught is that this particular education will provide such a wide range of knowledge and well-rounded skills that businesses will drool over you in an attempt to get such a qualified employee in the door. I still have my bib on to fight off the drool, but haven't had to use it just yet.

The myth goes on to claim that English majors can just continue their education and become educators themselves. Though this may in fact be true for some it is unlikely for many others, as I pointed out. Even if I were to gain the master's degree and wait to go further than that, my position as an adjunct faculty somewhere would condemn me to having to teach so many sections of composition per term that the hourly rate would sink to poverty levels. Even my professors who counseled me advised against this route.

I have to admit that I resented falling prey to the myth. I did everything that a student could do. I even went above and beyond. I won nearly every academic award available, I wrote and published for my university and even held office in the honor society. And now having done my best to promote the school, I was unemployed and nearly unemployable. I almost wanted to get back at academia as much as I wanted a writing job. I also remembered all those students who were not English majors who barely graduated because of their inability to express themselves in written form. The myth began to give way to opportunity. I returned to the computer, arbitrarily chose a service and clicked.

FraudPapers is the company I went with. O.K. I've got to be honest with you here. That may sound kind of funny coming from a forger who is holding a martini in one hand and typing with the other, but you've gotten this far with me so you might as well go ahead and keep trusting. As I noted in the Preface, FraudPapers isn't really their name. I'll just call it that for the purpose of our discussion. I mean, I wouldn't want to get shot or anything if they get genuinely grumpy with me for outing their business. That may sound strange and dramatic, too, but I'll clear that all up later, promise.

Anyhow, their site offered some good money if I was in fact a good writer. All I had to do was give them my credentials and a little writing sample and I'd be on my way. I sent a whole *curriculum vitae* along with a lengthy article I had previously written and waited. It sure didn't take long. They got back with me, congratulating me on my acceptance as a junior writer and reminding me to review all of their policies and procedures for becoming a successful writer with them. Before I did all that, though, I wanted to know one thing: how much money could I get?

That's the big issue, isn't it? I was mad at the system, and mad that I couldn't make good money in an aboveboard fashion, and now I just wanted to use my talents to make some cash. That's it. A few quick clicks brought me to the available orders page. As a junior level writer I didn't have access to many orders, and only basic ones at that. They did pay well, though, comparatively. Papers on such basic subjects as Shakespeare and English Literature paid anywhere from one dollar and sixty-six cents per page all the way up to two dollars and twenty-two cents a page. That may not sound like much, but considering what the freelancers' positions offered it looked heavenly. That's it. Foundation one of why academic forgery is on the rise in America is that there is a large class of disgruntled, highly-qualified writers who just can't make the living they anticipated.

Foundation Two: The Foreign Factor

The numbers of orders coming from obviously foreign students, or those for whom English is a second language, is startling. It is pretty difficult not to notice when looking at the order instruction pages. A lot of the clients make it clear up front that they do not speak English well at all. An instruction sheet might say, "Please to writer I am not speaking the English too good so don't be using but small words." I'm not kidding. These students need to pass college for whatever personal reasons they have for attending an American school, but they are savvy enough to realize that they have a problem in doing so. They must pass that dreaded English class but cannot do it on their own. However if they get a classmate to help them it would be too obvious and they would be detected. Therefore they go to a professional essay writing company like Fraud-

Papers to take care of this need. Presumably the staff writers are good enough to not only write a quality paper but have the ability to water down the language to at least make it seem possible, if not actually likely, that the client wrote the paper.

This can get downright complicated. I would end up having a client who wanted me to write personal responses to literature based upon his cultural upbringing. This required some initial research into just what his culture was like. I mean I can't just make that up. So there was a little time spent going back and forth on the company's messaging system until I had a good enough flavor of what it was like for him growing up in the family that he did. Then I could read the stories through his eyes and pretend to be him as I responded. There ought to be a bonus for that, but at the very least it is a tremendous amount of fun when it goes well.

I feel sorry for the pressures that these individuals are under. Generally speaking, they seem nice enough and hardworking enough. It is just that they have a family obligation to complete their education at this particular institution and they know that their chances of getting through the core curriculum are rather slim. They know that they will ultimately do well in their major curriculum, but the general education courses could prevent them from ever getting to that level. That must be very stressful and in the end they turn to forgers for their basic papers. The forgers do so and feel the satisfaction of knowing that their clients will be able to pursue their futures, along with the added joy of fooling another set of instructors. Forgery is a powerful addiction.

Foundation Three: Legacies and Losers

It is this category, along with foundation one, that gets right at the heart of just why academic forgery is on the rise in American educational institutions. It's a cultural thing. There is a growing and pervasive attitude of young people wanting to have the achievements without doing the work. They either don't want to, or think they are somehow above it. I call these groups legacies and losers. You find them everywhere.

1. Foundations for Forgery

I spent a lot of time, ironically, writing in college towns and on campuses. It is not that I would ever meet my clients face-to-face, as that is not allowed under any company's policy in this business (remember what I said about the slightly criminal underworld-ness of this job?), but there are advantages to those locales. First of all it put me close to research libraries in the event that I actually had to find a hard copy of something that is on the rare side. Second there are always academic textbook stores at hand which cover the newer editions of texts that seem to sprout up ubiquitously every semester. I couldn't just buy every new edition that came out, especially when the only differences primarily were different pagination which I would need for accurate citations. Picking up one of these tomes and briefly thumbing through it could give me what I needed in just a few minutes. Then it would go back on the shelf and I would go out the door.

The most valuable reason to me for writing in different college towns was the environment. It felt good to be on campus. Somehow it was even more empowering knowing that I was writing papers successfully for these places without having to follow their rules. I followed their rules previously and it didn't take me very far, so it became, "Now look what I can do. I really do belong. Take that." Also it put me into social contact with the college population and reminded me why I had so many orders at any one time. Take this restaurant/bar example:

It wasn't even the weekend yet and the place was packed. I'm sure that everyone was over twenty-one … well fairly sure. Anyway they were all students of the local school, that's for sure. I happened to know from their schedules (and some of my orders) that they really ought to be in the dorms studying and writing four- to six-page research papers. But instead they were here swilling beer (as opposed to sipping a martini) and partying raucously. The local football game was on the big screen and the talk was loud, loud, loud. It wasn't about academics. These were the people I worked for most often.

The group I call the legacies are those who approach their instructors with an incredulous look after receiving low grades on papers. They don't even bother being subtle. Professors tell me that they already know who these students are, because the students have made it clear from the beginning. The names of their family connections readily pour from

Section I: Studies in Forgery

their mouths like a thoroughbred's pedigree. They expect to receive good grades. They will receive good grades. Many of the professors actually give in because it is such an exasperation to fight back time and time again. The more upstanding among them refuse. They grade according to the effort and expertise of the paper. This infuriates the legacies who end up having to produce better papers. Often at the very last moment they then come to a service for a bailout. They are usually the huffy ones who place orders with the instructions that, "I need this right away—don't be late! My professor won't accept one more late paper!" The truly sad thing is that these are usually such simple papers. Nothing more than an analysis of a poem or a short story. I could get this done in under an hour, for a price. With that short of a deadline the price per page increases with the company. This doesn't seem to bother these sorts of clients who routinely put in late orders. I would write quickly and well, send it, get paid and never hear another word from the client until the next order.

Equally obnoxious are the plain lazy losers. These are the individuals that want all their papers done by someone else. They have found out that there is such a thing as a company like FraudPapers and they are bound and determined to use them to the max. They also made up the large portion of the above bar-hopping crowd, I'm sure. They don't seem fazed at the lateness of the hour or the fact that they probably have something due in the morning. The party goes on and on.

These clients live in the current culture of commercialism. Anything can be bought. It is a retail world. Like the legacies that expect their grades, the losers expect that they can simply buy their way through or out of things. By and large they are right. Our culture does support this type of behavior. Need a book? Check the online sales company. All the reviews are there, along with the edition options, the binding, etc. All shipped to your door. How about a movie? Just the same. What about an essay for your third period Anthropology class? Ossi Chesterton's your man. Just place the order and ante up the money. You'll even receive it faster than the movie you just ordered. Just pay and download. It will even be formatted for your particular instructor's needs. All you have to do is hit print. Oh yeah, and make sure that there is ink in your printer. That would be sad and would mean another trip to the Internet for a new cartridge twin pack.

Because of this culture of non-responsibility and general laziness, the numbers of clients for academic forgers continues to rise exponentially. This is also due to the cultural/social aspect. Remember what I said about the bar crowd? All of those patrons were students. All of them had papers due, presumably. That is where the sociology part of academic forgery comes in. Just like the word about a good party spreads, word spreads about a particular essay writing service. When someone has a good experience and gets a good grade and low stress for the money, they tend to tell their peers. Before long there are a large number of friends all using the same service and saving themselves a lot of time for partying during the week, even if it means that the papers cost them a few drinks' expense along the way.

Foundation Four: Businessmen Under Pressure

I've been thinking that this particular group supporting academic forgers is related to the previous one. I don't necessarily mean to imply that businessmen who use writing services are losers (or are losers anymore) but that they are now handicapped. Imagine a business major in college. He is so focused on business theories, management practices, and the like that he really cannot be bothered to achieve a quality level of writing. Eventually he graduates, after maybe using an essay writing service like FraudPapers to help with compositions, and enters the business world. All is well for a while. However, he gets promoted and the boss wants written reports, presentations and proposals. Now what? Mr. Businessman has the knowledge, undeniably, but cannot get the ideas to the page in any logical fashion. More than once I received orders in my box from these clients. I'd be presented with an overview of a company problem or a marketing idea and have to come up with the solution, in the proper format. Sometimes the client told me what the solution was, generally speaking, and I did the actual writing. More nefariously I was sometimes asked to fix the company problem myself in a proposal paper that then went to the board with the client's name at the top instead of mine, not that I would share mine anyway, but you get the idea. So while I might be sipping a martini here in my hometown, it was possible that a boss somewhere might be sipping one, say in Tacoma, reading my proposal and wondering if it would save his business. Funny thing, isn't it? It is really an eye opener to begin examining just why academic forgery is on the rise. These foundations represent those reasons in a nutshell.

Well, there it is, closing time for seminar one. Next time, we'll take a look at the liars, legacies, and losers that make up the orders upon which academic forgers live.

2

Liars, Legacies, and Losers

The Forger at Work: *It's Monday morning, and just like any upstanding employee in America I don't feel particularly motivated to work quite yet. It's not that I don't like what I do. On the contrary, forgery has really become fun. I'm making money, earning respect from my clients for my writing, which is important to my writer's ego, and simultaneously taking the occasional shot at university English departments across the country.*

Still, it's a Monday. As I pour my first coffee of the day, I log in. Ossi Chesterton is at work. Not wanting to wade through the order queue right now, I am rewarded by a peek into my inbox. There it is: an order from a loser. Good news.

Let me explain. I deal with three groups. They are liars, legacies, and losers. The first think they're not so bad, the second think they're absolutely great, and well, the last group … well let me tell you. The last group is where I make most of my money. They're my best friends. They keep me from having to look for orders and compete on bids with other writers. That's because the losers have me write everything, and I mean everything, they have to do in college. I write, they party. When I go down to the bar and grill on campus to write, I am most likely surrounded by those same clients. For fun, I try to match up the partiers with assignments that I have on my laptop screen. It's a fun game over a martini or two—my drink of choice. I wonder, as an aside, if a vodka company would consider sponsoring a forger. Probably not. Back to the losers.

These students were first-time customers of mine at one point, and they loved what they got from me. So much so that they asked for my writer number. That, by the way, is part of the fun of being a forger. It is almost like being a secret agent. There is nothing quite real about me. No one knows my name, except my personal account manager, and no one knows how else to contact me except through my writer identification number. So these customers of mine know me as Writer 76197. After their initial successes with my services, they now ask for me directly when they place orders. As a result, their orders come straight to my inbox instead of to the ever growing general orders database. This treatment, of course, comes with a price. There is a premium to having one's own writer. This is the domain of the losers.

Hence the e-mail in front of me. It reads much like the rest of this ilk. "Dear Writer 76197. Got your paper for my history class and it did great. Another 'A.' Next is just like that one. It's supposed to be a compare/contrast of the main generals of the civil war. Both sides. I guess like Lee and Grant, but maybe even more? I don't know. I'm sure that you have some in mind. So, like 3–5 pages with a good intro and conclusion, MLA, everything like the last. Thanks!" I'll try not to get offended by the reminder to use MLA and of course include the intro and conclusion. I take a brief look at the instruction particulars. Typical loser order. Because he has no plans to do any of his work on his own, he is organized. I'm surprised he hasn't sent a syllabus. Some do. Needless to say, though, I could figure it out if I were that interested, which I'm not. Every order has a ten day deadline, the format is always the same. One after another.

So I have a template for this particular client. I open my documents folder, find the file and voilá, the last essay comes up. I change the date and come up with a snappy title. Competing Battles, Competing Generals. *Kind of corny, but it will suffice. I leave the "Your Name Here" line highlighted to remind said customer to add that particular when he turns it in. Then I'm off to the races. One more cup of coffee, a few open book-marked tabs that I take most of my history research from, and I dive in.*

Forty minutes later and one more paper for a loser is finished. Five more ticks of the clock and I have it proofed and the citations checked. All is in order. I add my personal notes to the client, making certain to remind him to send his client evaluation which will mean more money for me, and tap "submit."

I never had any intention of spending ten days, not to mention ten hours, on such a simple paper.

It's funny to me now that I think of it that the words "submit button" and "smug" both begin with the letter "s." Now that my Monday has gotten off to a good start and I'm feeling good about myself I can dig in to the orders queue and find higher value assignments. There have to be some last-minute pleas from the legacy group. Short deadlines come with bigger paychecks.

Seminar: It might seem that just as all forgers swim out of the same stream, their clients would as well. Cheaters are cheaters, right? Before I began writing for FraudPapers I believed this, too. It turns out that there are actually subtle nuances to this underground business world. I found that I could identify three distinct categories of clients: liars, legacies, and losers.

The first group, the liars, are those most associated by the common person as the "normal" cheaters. When asked in discussion groups who they think buys papers online, respondents routinely identify this sort of student. The perception is that there is probably cheating going on in college. Further, there must be people in classes that are tempted to get some help on a last-minute assignment. By and large this is correct. There are tremendous numbers of these students who make up a large percentage of academic forgery's clientele. Everyone knows that college is a busy time for students. This is especially true now that the majority of enrollees are concurrently working at least a part-time job while they are attempting to complete their studies. As college becomes more expensive and sometimes outruns inflation, and as grants and scholarships are beginning to dry up somewhat, undergraduates are faced with two primary choices. They can take out loans. Many do. However, students are growing savvy and they're not immune to the news. The words "student loans" and "saddled with debt" are often found running together in headlines. So an increasing number of collegiates are beginning to feel wary of borrowing against their education. The second option is to work. Sometimes part-time, often full-time, the days become very long. They are also difficult to manage. Work schedules have to be arranged around class schedules, and vice versa. Some employers are more flexible than others when it comes to this. Either way, the days are full and lengthy. With little time for traditional study groups and late-night cram sessions, students occasionally (and not so occasionally, as I will point out later) run out of time to write their papers. They then are faced with two more choices. First, the paper can be turned in late. This only works if the professor will take late papers. Even if accepted, however, the grade is usually lowered due to the tardiness of the effort. To some, this is acceptable. To others, the answer is to buy a paper quickly.

But to whom shall they turn? The problem is that they really can't go to another student in their class. There are simply too many complications with that. To begin with, the other students are presumably just as busy as the one facing this dilemma. They have similar course loads, jobs, etc. They can't be approached. This doesn't even begin to take into consideration the fact that the students in question may actually turn down the request because of their own moral code, or fears that they may be caught, which could jeopardize their own academic future. It may seem unlikely that this situation, i.e., one student turning to another, ever occurs. The truth is, it doesn't, according to my research. However, at the same time, I often get asked this when I introduce the concept of students cheating, plagiarizing, or outright buying their essays. "Don't they (the cheaters) go to someone else in the class and borrow their research or notes?" is the common inquiry. Absolutely not.

The thought of that as a solution doesn't give today's students, especially the devious ones, enough credit. This is the Internet era. College kids are more aware than ever that there are easy ways to cheat with much less risk and liability. They're not stupid. Going to one of their peers not only opens them up to possible plagiarism charges, but runs contrary to all of the crime dramas that fill much of the television schedules today. Everyone seems to know that the easiest way to get turned in is for a partner in crime to turn on them. Best not to leave these obvious loopholes.

Perhaps someone from another section of the course could bail the student out. There are many offerings of ENG 101 and the like across the school day. At any one time at some schools, three to five different instructors are covering this general education requirement. This would appear to be a safer endeavor, although it requires some strong networking skills. Either the other student could write the paper, again keeping the above restrictions and roadblocks in mind, or a few paragraphs could be copied and pasted from them. The thinking is that the papers would never cross each other or end up in the same inbox or stack on a desk. That may be right, actually. Again, perhaps not strangely, many nonstudents I talk to think that this is what academic forgery is all about. This approach, though, is problematic, too. There is always the chance, no matter how slim, that a professor or teaching assistant discovers the plagiarism. English departments are usually not so big that the professors don't ever talk about their courses. This is especially true of those teaching the prerequisites. Many times the faculty in question are adjunct or lecturers. These employees are among the most frustrated of staff in colleges today. They are paid much less than their peers who hold a Ph.D. and they are usually tasked to teach many sections of introductory English each and every term. They are more likely to vent their woes with other similar teachers. It is certainly not outside the realm of possibility for two or three to gather at the local coffee shop and shower each other with stories of, "I can't believe this stuff I'm grading. Look at this one, and this." And then maybe, just maybe, one of them has a moment of realization that this looks familiar. The matches discovered, it is just a matter of grabbing the cheaters for a little office session. Both students would then face probation or expulsion. But just to shed some light on the odds of all that happening, I should point out that I have never heard of it taking place. The simple and elegant solution for ne'er do wells to avoid all of these hassles is to seek out an online service.

Just as easily as I found a company to work for, any student can search for a paper to buy. Going to the most common search engine right now and typing the outright blatant words "buy an essay" results in over 200,000,000 entries. Needless to say, not all of these listings are for students seeking papers for purchase. In fact, the fifth one in order on my latest search describes why a student should not engage in this activity. Before and after that, however, are sponsored ads and entries entreating those interested to use their "24/7 services." Also found are provisions for guaranteed quality, assignments written by expert writers, all original essays, and perhaps best of all, cheap essays! Keep in mind, this is only the first page of results. That accounts for approximately 12 possible places to order from per search page. With over 16,000,000 pages after that one, it would seem that the companies seeking placement on that first list would have to spend some good money to get there.

Even typing in a much narrower search to ensure the student only gets results directly relating to contacting a paper mill, e.g. "essay writing services" yields over 43,000,000 hits in a little over a quarter of a second. When I share this with those I speak to and survey regarding how they perceive buying essays in school, I get blank stares. I'm often asked, "No, really? That can't really be true." That is exactly why I bring my laptop to these sessions. I pretend to be a needy student looking for a break and some help. I show groups just how easy it is to get in touch with these organizations. Even taking the time to choose a company and fill out an online order form after registering, creating a password and everything, generally takes under five minutes. It usually takes longer to wait for the billing department to confirm the method of payment. All told, I demonstrate, I can order a paper in under fifteen minutes. Back to the students who are doing these searches.

The easiest papers to find are often the exact papers that simple liars need. For as much as the services make themselves sound like experts in the field writing difficult papers, the truth of the matter is that nearly everything produced falls into the introductory, general education coursework. That is because those are the products that the majority of the clients need. It is a retail business. If a car dealership sells more of their middle-range sedans than their flashy sports cars, the lot will be predominately filled with those sedans. The same with the forgery business.

Therefore, essays covering classical literature, reviews of basic dramas and the like are all available for ten bucks or so and a click. The liars order these papers and justify their actions to themselves and the forgers that it is just one paper for one not-so-very important class, and leave it at that. Unwittingly, they are supporting the vast number of the forgers' lifestyles. The paradox here is that liars really don't think that badly of themselves. The typical cheater believes, whether true or not, that they are just going to do this one time. It's not even as if it's an important class or paper. Despite this, the order comments often show an awareness of wrongdoing. Comments such as, "I don't usually have problems with these kinds of things, but this one has me stumped," or, "I am so busy this semester and have so much work, I just need this one paper," indicate some guilt. This is funny. These forms of revelation are only designed to make the liar feel better about himself. The forger could not possibly care less, and only finds it amusing that the client is trying to get him to not judge the customer harshly, or think that he is a bad person. The forger, judging the moral tenets of the customer? Really? He is forging a paper, after all. Ethics are not considerations of either party.

Then there are the legacies. These students are difficult for everyone to handle. They approach their instructors with an absolutely incredulous look after receiving a low grade on a paper. Not even bothering to be subtle, they thrust the paper into the instructors' faces and often just look at them. Professors have told me that they already know who these students are, because the pupils in question approach them early in the semester and make it clear that good grades will be given their papers. Period. Sometimes it is a coy little game. "Hello, Professor Smith," they begin. "I am so glad to meet you. My father is one of the regents of the university and he has talked about you often. He really respects your methods, and I am looking forward to being in your class this term." One can almost hear the "wink, wink" that is going on here. Other times, it is pure, distilled, and blunt. There is no wink. They expect to receive good grades. They will receive good grades.

Many of the instructors actually give in at this point, because it is such an exasperation to fight back time and time again. The distraction inherent in challenging this so often takes valuable time, and stress, and keeps them from spending quality time and office hours helping other students who are actually trying hard to learn.

The more upstanding of the staff refuse to play this game. They grade each and every paper from each and every student the same. Effort and expertise earn high grades, and poor submissions receive poor ones. That makes sense, doesn't it? This infuriates the legacies who are faced with low marks and the need to produce better work. If their attempts to mediate the situation with another visit to the office don't change things, then a new tack needs to be taken.

Often, at the very last moment the legacy comes to a forger for help. These orders are usually the ones accompanied with the instructions and comments such as, "I need this right away—don't be late! My professor will not accept a late paper. And it better be good because I need an 'A'!"

The truly sad thing is that these are usually such simple papers. Nothing more than an analysis of a poem or a short story. A forger can get this type of thing done in under an hour, for a price. With that short of a deadline, the price per page increases. The client is not necessarily told this. They only receive the dollar amount due with the order. The forgers know, though.

Section I: Studies in Forgery

When a writer logs into his order queue, the first thing he looks for is an icon that represents a high-value order. It may be because of the very short deadline, or it may be due to a complicated, lengthy assignment. Within a few seconds, the forger knows which scenario it is. If it is due to the time constraint, it becomes of valuable interest. This is especially true of the legacies' purchases. A typical order may be for a topic such as "analyze the tragic elements of Hamlet." The price per page may have increased threefold, and yet the order is so simple! A click, a chuckle, and the forger has just taken in a nice and easy paycheck.

The price doesn't seem to bother this sort of client, who routinely puts in these late orders. Never did I receive a comment or question about the cost of a paper from a customer whom I deemed to fall into the legacy category. I simply wrote quickly and fairly well, sent it, got paid, and never heard another word from them.

Even more obnoxious to the forger is the last group. These are the plain lazy losers. They are the individuals that want all their papers done by someone else. They literally make a career out of finding people to take care of their course loads. It has occurred to them that there is such a thing as a company like FraudPapers, and they are bound and determined to use them to the max.

This is arguably the most disturbing side of the forgery business. It is definitely the most blatant. I expect that readers may find it also the most surprising. The concept that there may be students in schools today that do not complete any of their own academic work is stunning, and difficult to believe. Yet, it is true.

Therefore, it is not difficult to assign them the categorical title of lazy losers. To think of these students as anything but lazy is irrational. Likewise, the rather colloquial term of loser. I think that most of society would accept that nomenclature. My research has indicated that these clients operate in two ways. First are the ones that are seeking to get their papers done for as cheaply as possible.

I often encountered orders completely separate from each other that I have taken over a period of time that had identically-worded instructions. Keep in mind that these were not the instructions from instructors' syllabi (although I came across that many times, too). Further, the timetables and expectations from the orders were also identical.

Usually they were very well planned out. The deadlines were about ten days or so, indicative of seeing the course schedule at the beginning of the term and planning each paper accordingly.

Similarly, the price per page would be set at the lowest rung. Because they were such easy papers, writers would pick them up quickly, especially the junior writers who didn't have access to more difficult orders, and so they never grew in price. They were taken by the company, completed early and sent back to the customer who would send along another paper shortly thereafter. In that manner, obnoxious doesn't describe their behavior. They were very hands-off clients. The exchange of orders and papers went expediently and easily. There was a nice structure to these students' needs. The aforementioned adjective "obnoxious" applies to the more objective, societal look and impression surrounding them. Whether they were difficult to deal with, or not, the fact remains that most of their undergraduate work, maybe even their entire degree, was purchased. This applies to the other facet of this sect, too.

For every loser that seeks to sweep up their papers for as cheaply as possible to keep their career of purchasing their degree alive, there is another who sets out to learn everything they can about the company's writers and standards before committing to this long-term fraud. Of course, the instant thought that comes to mind is, if they only turned their hard work and research to the powers of good … cliché but true! Most often, these customers have already networked with other students who use the service (more about that later) and know which writer to trust their papers to. Yes, they know their writers.

Imagining this shopping around part of the business really opens minds to the cultural aspect of academic forgery. It is just as much a retail environment as knowing which supermarket has the best produce, or which restaurant has the best service. Once this is considered, it becomes easier to understand how it is that forgers thrive. Students that have no intention of doing their own writing over much of their undergraduate time may be aware that it would best behoove their charade if all of their assignments are standardized in their authorial voice, writing style, format and structure. It would be far more difficult to point the finger at them, or even have doubts as to the provenance of their work, if nothing seemed amiss on its face. As a result, once a customer receives a paper from a company that really satisfies them, and which receives an acceptable grade, he makes sure to notate the writer number of the forger. These employee numbers are displayed in lieu of actual names and contact information. This allows for customers to communicate directly with their writers when concerns or questions arise. More often, however, the numbers are used to create follow-up orders. The next time that a customer needs an order fulfilled, he just enters the writer's number in the proper box on the electronic form. The order itself then never shows up in the general queue from which all of the writers of appropriate level may review it and take it. Instead, it is earmarked for and directly sent to the inbox of the specific writer requested. This is good for everyone, the client, the writer, and the company.

The client benefits from the belief that he will not get caught, for the above mentioned reasons. Especially if the student takes several courses with the same instructor, this confidence is paramount. In addition, it serves to provide the student with a sense of order. The loser-type customer is absolutely reliant on the fact that his writer will come through for him each and every time, and on schedule. With any luck at all, his servant is skilled in all of the classes that come up. This is key to this form of loser.

It is also beneficial to the writer. The forger wants two things out of his business. First, a steady stream of orders is a must. One of the reasons they got into this community was to avoid being an unemployed writer. Being an unemployed forger is just as bad. And there really is no going to the unemployment office with a note saying that you lost your academic forgery job, is there? A regular customer can keep his writer busy for literally years. To make a good living, the writer would also need to maintain a good relationship with the order queue, but it is a great start. The second thing that the forger wants is a life without hassles. Many clients can be very difficult to deal with. They may have attitudes right off the get go, like the legacy who wants his good grade or else. They might have unreasonable expectations such as wanting papers to include a pattern of two short sentences for every long one. Or they could continue asking for revisions over and over until the writer meets all of the additional concerns or the company cuts the customer off. Return customers eliminate those problems. The writer knows what to expect, and most likely has saved the template from these orders to make everything go smoothly and easily. The writing itself goes very quickly, then, and paychecks are realized without much effort or thought. Then there is the additional bonus of not having to look through the database for an order ... it's already right there and waiting in the inbox.

It's obvious why this circumstance is beneficial to the company itself. As with any retail business, satisfied customers who return provide a steady flow of income. Marketing opportunities are rather limited when it comes to essay writing businesses. Beyond good search engine optimization and word-of-mouth, there is not much a company can do to increase business. The lazy loser who finds a writer he loves to deal with a multitude of times guarantees ongoing revenue.

Finally, there is one last benefit to both the company and the writer in question. There is a cost to the customer for finding and selecting his favorite forger. To guarantee the order goes to his chosen writer, a premium is added to the cost. Although this may seem like a perk that regular customers earn, it is really extortion by the company itself. It is not stated this way, but the mandate is clear: either pay up or we'll send your paper to someone that may not do the job you expect. The lazy loser generally opts for the price increase to eliminate worries. Again, everyone's happy.

That is the basic breakdown of the types of students that seek, and therefore support, the business of academic forgery. They really do represent the growing awareness of commercialism in American society, and so it shouldn't come as a surprise that they look much like shoppers found in every store across the land. In the next seminar, one additional sector will be added to the mix: the foreign factor.

3

The Foreign Factor

The Forger at Work: *One of the most entertaining of challenges I've faced so far in the world of academic forgery is the language issue. Allow me to stop for a minute. I am not referring to the obvious, which would be making sure that my language is academic in nature, not repetitive, and that sort of thing. I'm really not talking about style whatsoever, in its traditionally understood college rhetorical sense. What I'm referring to is trying to make believe that I have the same grasp of the English language as a student who does not speak English as their first language.*

Case in point. There's an order in front of me right now with very limited instructions. I'm thinking that this could be a good thing. The client may not be one of the more needy ones that has dozens of details that he would like to see attended to. The standard wording is all there on the screen. Paper level: undergraduate. Topic: English. Subject: drama. Length: 2–3 pages. Style: MLA. Then it hits me. There is a special request line. It reads, "Please to writer not make hard English I will fail again!" Poor William Shakespeare is about to be covered in "not too hard the English." I do hope the bard is not offended, or rolling in his grave. This is a bit like analyzing the classics, thinking analytically, and then boiling it all down to a picture book. Another way I see it is like trying to write subtitles for a movie that I am watching in my mind. The words that I would normally find on the blackboard in my head are merely synonyms for what I will ultimately type on the screen, therefore. I try to drink coffee instead of martinis while working on these ones.

With enough patience and caffeine, I can write the paper in my head and translate it poorly to the paper. I am not being judgmental, here. I don't think that the student in question is dumb, or even educationally challenged. Purely by default, he must fall into one of the three categories of clients somewhere, but whether liar, legacy, or loser, he isn't worse than any of the non–ESL ones. Notwithstanding this fact, I'm not making a personal opinion call whatsoever. For all I know, this cheater is much smarter than I am. I just have language and leverage on my side. My professors once told me that I would find many applications for my linguistic learning. I bet they didn't have this in mind. I can now write in at least two accents.

That's just it, too. It's not about using bad language, or outright incorrect language. These students are in college and got there somehow. Outside of the English classes that are required, they could be experts in their fields. It's not like they can't write at all. They just don't use English outside the school environment. It's got to be frustrating, right? This is a great opportunity for me to build some contacts, here. If I get this right I would bet that not only could I do more papers for him, many more if he is an actual loser, but I'm sure that he would pass on my name (all right, my number) to his friends who might have the same circumstances. Ossi Chesterton, forger for the foreigners. Nice. Back to the details. I have to determine what the client's level of expertise is. Sometimes it is just a matter of not using the twenty-five cent words in academia, and sticking to the more mundane, five-centers. Sometimes it is a matter of working with the arrangement of the words, structurally. That may mean moving verbs to the end of the sentence. Somehow, all of this has to be extrapolated from a few lines of instruction on an order form. The assignment in front of me is a bit of a conglomeration of the two situations, I determine. Maybe I should take another, closer look at what I've put down before sending it.

One of my first thoughts for a topic sentence on this one was "The antagonist Iago in Shakespeare's Othello *idealizes evil in the extreme through his manipulation of others." That became "The character Iago in Shakespeare's* Othello *represents evil through manipulation." What I end up typing is "Iago in Shakespeare's* Othello *is most evil being manipulative." That will do.*

It is much like writing three papers. Sentence by sentence I see. Word by word I weave. Truncation by truncation I type.

Eventually a three page paper sits in front of me. At an added cost to my own personal funds I printed it out and have a red pen next to me. Oh yes, the dreaded red pen. I find that when trying to get one of these assignments "just so" it is easiest to be able to see it in hard copy form. If I need to rearrange things or see repetition that even outweighs the alleged writer's limitations, the scrawl of red arrows is easier to edit from than doing the same on my computer which doesn't show the whole document all at once. I'm pretty happy with the effort and play professor for a second: I see myself receiving the paper in person. The student looks familiar to me but he doesn't talk much in class. He's probably here on a student visa and isn't comfortable with the language yet. A quick glance at the first page confirms this. It's what I expect and return my smile to the unknown pupil. All is well and I'll try to be a little understanding and even forgiving when giving him a grade.

That's likely what is going to happen with this order in a few days.

These papers really ought to be worth more money. My opinion is that it is three times the work and should reap three times the pay. The client's thoughts are that it is just a simple paper for a freshman class and should be cheap. FraudPapers rules that it is somewhere in between the two.

I want to be a raise needing.

Seminar: The foreign factor comprises a significant part of the academic forgery market in America. It is not difficult to see why. By and large, these students are in the United States on student visas and they are not majoring in English language and literature. Many, too, are not planning on staying in the country at the end of their studies. Because of this, a large number of this group do not have a strong interest in mastering the nuances of the language. Generally speaking, this is not a huge problem. There is no requirement of them to do so. Unless a student is concerned with receiving all "A" grades during his time at the university, there is no reason to become too stressed out by introductory classes' writing needs. A passing grade of any sort will do. All majors pursued have restrictions to their entry, but receiving the highest accolades in writing is not usually one of them.

In addition, many professors are surprisingly forgiving when it comes to these students' efforts. It is a form of reverse prejudice, of sorts. During my research I discovered that when instructors read papers that are written in clearly halting language—but not outright incorrect language—they very often look at the name of the student. If it is manifest that the writer is a foreign national, the benefit of the doubt rule applies. This is a poor system full of loopholes, both positive and negative. It is not fair to American students who speak the language fluently. It is overly generous to American students who do not have a mastery of the language for cultural reasons. Foreign students are favorably excused. The list goes on and on. It is just plain wrong. As with most situations, it is really the academic forger who benefits.

There are two primary situations in which forgers encounter foreign clients. For the purpose of discussion, by the way, the term foreigners or foreign clients can apply to American citizens who are raised in a tight-knit culture that precludes the use of English as a first language. This does not imply that they are not really Americans or are second-class citizens. It only comments on their mastery and skills in using the written English language to express themselves. The most basic circumstance is when these non-native speakers, or their foreign national counterparts, need general education papers to be written.

These assignments can be essays on rhetoric, such as exposition or analysis, which make up the meat of freshman level English courses. They also may be similar assignments in introductory social sciences classes like psychology, philosophy, etc. Anything closely resembling the five paragraph essay falls into this category. What is ambiguous or at least difficult to grasp is just why the student is in the position of ordering papers from mills. Are they good students who are merely liars or losers, or are they actually needier when it comes to language and therefore perhaps more, dare it be said, justified in their using a paper writing service? Forgers as a whole do not care, but it makes for a fascinating discussion and applies to the business of forgery itself. Should this entire class of clients be viewed favorably or given some level of forgiveness straight away?

The easiest answer to this question is that no, they do not deserve more consideration than any other cheater. Just because they are non-native speakers does not give them any more right to turn in a paper that they did not write as do any of their peers. It is most probable, in fact, to assume that all of these cheaters, whether they are doing it one time or many, are doing so for all of the same reasons. They may be downright unethical in their mores, they may justify their actions as being overwhelmed by college life, or it could be just a onetime giving in to temptation. In this manner, a cheat is a cheat is a cheat, whatever category he may fall into.

It is absolutely imperative that instructors of all levels in post-secondary education assume that their students have a firm grasp of the English language. Colleges have requirements for entry, not hopeful standards. For someone to have made it to the collegiate realm, he must have previously completed primary and secondary courses which necessitated command of writing skills. Standardized testing used to gain entrance to universities also demand this ability. That is a good number of hurdles in the way of someone wanting to receive a degree in any field. Therefore all students should be able to be graded on the same coursework using the same standards. There is no inherent unfairness at play here. Consider the following circumstances:

Student A is a native speaker of English. He sits near the back of the class and the professor knows him because of his loud voice and somewhat inappropriate comments. He appears to be the stereotypical student that the teacher has discovered is common for the local school system to churn out. The first week, he turns in a paper that is poorly written. It analyzes the material fairly well, and is structured appropriately. The citations are correct and the format is right. However, the writing itself is atrocious. There are numerous misspellings, subject-verb agreement is wrong, and word choice itself is at times inaccurate. The instructor gives the paper a failing grade.

Student B strikes the instructor as much different. This pupil has talked to the professor before and obviously has difficulty with English. He speaks haltingly and his speech frequently misses prepositions; his use of tense is not always appropriate. When Student B submits the same assignment as Student A, it is very similar in its accomplishments. Fair analysis, right format, proper citations. The writing lacks clarity, however, and the grammar reflects his poor use of English. Ironically, Student A's paper showed these same failings. The instructor in question opts to focus on the depth and quality of analytical thinking in Student B's essay, and gives him a slightly passing grade.

Why?

It really doesn't matter why this is. Speculation can run rampant here regarding this situation. The bottom line is that it happens. Professors in several institutions have reported this to me over the course of my investigations. Most of them simply shrugged when I asked about the disparity and said it comes down to effort, sometimes. I disagree. In the above scenario, both students appear to have given the same effort and achieved the same results. The only difference was in the perception of the professor, and the grade given. In many cases, the non-native speaker counts on this awareness and understanding. Forgers absolutely count on it.

If this weren't so, then this type of client would demand much more of their writers. If they were held to the same standard as the native speakers in the class, then the instructions on the orders to FraudPapers would not read, "Do not make the English too hard." This shows an awareness by the client of the fact that professors will, in fact, pass their papers despite not-so-good language skills. Moreover, they know that something written too well would only stand out. It's not worth the risk.

Another common situation in which forgers encounter foreign clients, though fortunately less common than the above, occurs when students need to analyze or interpret a piece of writing through the lens of their own upbringing or cultural view. It is unclear just why these assignments come to forgers, because it is somewhat unclear as to why the assignments are given, in the first place. This type of order is fairly commonplace, and always comes from non-native speakers of English. In my experience with academic forgery outlets, I have never once come across this request from a student whose first language is English. Where, then, are these coming from? If they were assigned in typical courses at American institutions, it is unthinkable that native speakers' orders never came through the portal at FraudPapers. What is most likely is the orders are coming from overseas schools or schools that exist for the purpose of educating foreign nationals at American schools. The classes are entirely made up of non-native speakers who must use the English language when earning their degrees, for whatever reason that may be. This is one of the only explanations that is rational. Occasionally, this belief is bolstered by a mistake on the part of the client who fails to omit school information from the scanned-in class instruction sheet or syllabus. Over time, two countries from Southwest Asia pop up in this manner quite often.

How do forgers manage to succeed with this type of paper? Without having lived in the client's culture and upbringing, it should be impossible. But there are two reasons why the writers can do this. The first relates to all forms of forgery's clientele. Succinctly, the literature underlying the assignment is usually just basic in nature. Shakespeare, Dickens, and Molière come up as often in these schools as they do the ones on American soil. Basic English courses are all the same. Because of this, the forger who remains busy has a head start on almost anything that he will see. Even more helpful is the fact that forgers all have the ability to see the assignment instruction sheet and order comments before he commits to the job. No forger likes to get in over his head on something because it may result in a revision request, which then must be completed for no extra money. What is more impressive, or disgusting perhaps, is that there is really a double forgery going on with these assignments.

As pointed out previously, forgers want a hassle-free career. They do not welcome revisions or pressure from anything else than the deadline clock. As a result, the writer not only creates the paper from scratch but also creates the cultural upbringing or home experience himself, as well. This is not as difficult as it sounds, and really isn't much extra work, either. It is a matter of coming up with a "voice" for the narrator of the paper. Even non-fiction papers have narrators when penned by a forger—it is his voice doing the talking. The forger counts on the fact that someone ordering a paper to turn in probably doesn't interact with the instructor all that often. The instructor is at a tremendous disadvantage. If the forger decides that it would be easier to analyze a personal reflection on Ernest Hemingway's "Hills Like White Elephants" through the eyes of a student that comes from a large family where children are valued above all else, then so be it. On the other hand, if he would be more comfortable analyzing this from the point of view of one who is an only child, then that becomes the angle. This is the forgery behind the forgery. Once this is decided, then the paper becomes quick and easy. As long as the instructor doesn't know the student personally, there will be no problems.

It is easy to feel compassion for a percentage of the foreigners that come to forgers for papers. Some make it clear in their instructions that they absolutely need to complete their education and get their degree so that they can earn enough money in their job to support an extended family. Many times it goes as far as needing to support not just the family here, but overseas, and may even be the method by which an entire community may be supported. The paper orders are very often accompanied by a lot of special comments in the requests section of the order form.

3. The Foreign Factor

Unlike typical forger fodder, though, these instructions are really more personal comments and revelations than anything else. Rarely, in fact, do they have much to do with the paper, at all. This is really peculiar to this type of client. Generally, when the parameters are entered into the form, the customer stops there and expects that the paper will be workable. This is excepting, of course, those who provide comments such as just what level of English wording they need to see in the essay. The comments box then relates the experiences of the client—what brought him to this point. Sometimes the course of their family trajectory is described. Often, the family has been in America for quite some time and this student is expected to go to college, get a degree, and grasp a piece of the American pie. Through this accomplishment, the immediate family and future generations will benefit. That is a lot of pressure on one person. It is not difficult to understand why this may influence the student to seek help on language-related problems. As described above, it may be purely financial more than anything. Apart from any flights of fancy regarding the American Dream, it is all about getting done with school, getting a better job as a result, and then sending the money to the circle of the family in an attempt to break the cycle they have been in.

Others still send in orders from a more legacy sort of foreign client. Usually these students are overseas and attend schools that are American run, or are preparatory schools for American university education. The families of these students send them for their education and expect them to achieve. Not just to pass. The reputation of the family name is on the line, and they expect good grades. They will get good grades. Sounds familiar, doesn't it? Nearly always, the syllabus or actual class information is sent with the instruction sheet, which is strange, to say the least. Forgers are discouraged by their companies from discovering anything whatsoever about the customers, and the reverse flow of personal information (back to the client) is actually forbidden. However, this section of the foreign factor sends the coursework as is, seemingly disinterested if anyone else knows, or as some forgers have speculated, the students are actually proud of the upper echelon education they are receiving. Now that is ironic.

A great deal of this latter component of customers attends secondary educational institutions overseas. They are boarding prep schools.

Section I: Studies in Forgery

In essence, the clients are at the same level in their education and physical/mental development as American high schoolers. That they are under this amount of pressure already in their young lives underscores just how much additional pressure will be placed upon them as they rise to the ranks of post-secondary education student, and maybe even masters students or doctoral candidates at some point. What is vital to understand about the foreign factor and the facts behind this group as a whole is that these are not guesses or stereotypical assumptions. The comments and requests described come from the research files of academic forgery. They are among the easiest of pieces of the puzzle to ferret out, in fact. That is because the foreign factor utilizes company communication tools more than any other sector in this retail business. Think of it as the customer service department. Those who do not speak English as a first language are not reluctant to express themselves in writing, strangely enough.

Most other clients simply place orders, leave few comments in the requests boxes and pay up when the essay is sent to them. Unless they become repeat business for the company, the forger will never hear from them again. With the foreign language clients the situation is different. They can, and do, send the forger messages before, during, and fairly often after, the process. These e-mails are chock full of personal information. Really, they are narratives. Especially in the case of a customer needing a paper from a certain cultural background's point of view, many details are shared. Before long, even over the course of a short project the forger starts feeling like a part of the extended family. Sometimes they are told what the names of the siblings, parents, and such are so that these details can be added to the paper. Living conditions are described as well as the environment of the city or country in which they live. It can be quite the large amount of data—even more than the research a writer will put into the work. This is really not good for the academic forger, and is detrimental to the efforts of American academia to stop academic forgery as a whole. That is because in addition to the quality, disenfranchised writers' desires to get back at the system that put them into this predicament, they now have an even stronger value that can be put on and hidden behind to excuse their actions.

The forger begins to believe that they are helping needy students to aid their even needier families and friends.

3. The Foreign Factor

Academic forgers usually do not talk about their work. I have not encountered the situation even once where a group of people met in a bar, greeted each other with the traditional, "So what do you do?" and had the answer come back, "Oh, I'm an academic forger. You?" This is not because the practice itself is illegal. It is because whether they admit it to anyone else other than themselves these formerly distinguished academicians feel shame about what they do. As much as they know it isn't against the law and therefore they will never be indicted for their work, they always know—are always aware—that what they are engaging in is fraud. Pure and simple. Nothing can happen to them now, but if they were the students they were helping, the circumstances would be vastly different. Their vaunted education would go down the drain. They would be called into the professor's office, at best. At worst, they would be subject to an academic ethics committee hearing and punished for the violations. This very well could mean expulsion from the university itself, and even having their access to other institutions barred for a long time. It is the ultimate public dunce's cap. Every forger thinks about this at least once in a while, though far more frequently than confessed, I would state. The practice of assisting English as a second language students to gain a foothold in society helps make this all better. It may sound preposterous, but it is true, nonetheless.

It is really a grand game of make-believe for someone already engaged in make-believe for a business venture. Especially helpful to maintain this charade is the fact that these foreign factor clients are usually much less demanding than their native-speaking peers. There are not as many revisions, and most of the communication back and forth involves personal information like background, as opposed to the communication from the "typical" liars, legacies, and losers who tend to whine and nit-pick at times. I think that there is a much more heightened awareness of two things which account for this finding.

To begin with, a lot of the exchange of e-mails between client and forger in these cases includes apologetic language. There is apparently a more developed sense of humility and shame surrounding these students' needs to buy assistance. It is not unheard of to see sentences such as, "If my family were to know, I would be humiliated." Or, "I just need this one thing, and then never again." Because of this display of at least a modicum of integrity, there appears to be much more transparency and relationship building during the whole transaction. At least partially because of this, the forger feels better about helping this type of person. They do not seem like bad people, maybe just someone stuck in a very difficult situation. They are not hard to deal with, and so it seems less than just a business proposition, but somehow a more upstanding endeavor. Maybe not one that society would understand, but it helps soothe the feelings of the forger.

In addition, the whole lie that forgers tell themselves about how they are helping these families to rise above their situations and move upward in life is important. These are the writers who one can just imagine think of themselves as a proper organization akin to a United Nations relief agency, or some non-governmental organization that assists the world's needy. Perhaps this consortium could be called "Forgers Without Borders." As silly as this whole thing sounds to those outside of the business of academic forgery, this is probably the most important part of the discussion when it comes to the foreign factor. It is not just that they are a group of clients that come to the writers for papers. It isn't that they collectively support the business and create fairly good earnings for the individuals and the companies for whom they write. Instead, it is the fact that this group as a whole achieves something for the forger that nothing else quite can do. They make the academic forger feel good about himself. They assuage his worries. They alleviate if not eliminate self-doubts and perhaps self-loathing. The foreign-speaking clients are imperative to keeping the best of the forgers in business. As a result, they can be assigned the responsibility for keeping the best-of-the-best forgeries in the market. No former star of any undergraduate department in America, and especially a potential star of the writing pantheon, wants to be forging academic papers for a living. That is the plain and simple truth of the matter. Forgers want to be great writers of their own accord. They do not want writers' code numbers, hidden e-mail and payment accounts, and the inability to share with their classmates at reunions just what it is they do for a living. They definitely don't want to hear, "Hey, how's that writing career of yours going? Got a book deal yet?"

The foreign factor makes all of these things disappear for a while.

4

Honest Cheats, Career Cheaters, and Cheater Networks

The Forger at Work: *It's just me, myself, and I sitting in one of my favorite writing haunts, a small, locally owned and operated coffee shop. The three of us, my multiple personalities, are all busy. I'll explain. I found some time ago that several students who have used my services occasionally in the past are in the very same class. In fact, they are not only in the same class, but the same course, the same level, and the same section. In other words, in this situation I have three carbon copy orders. What's even funnier is that one of them forgot to delete the class information, and all three left their names on the assignment sheets. Thus, I know exactly for whom I am working. I know who the students are by name, who their professor is by name, and at which particular institution they can all be found. Thanks to the syllabus, I even know the time of day they meet, and which classroom in which building the class is taught. If I had any questions, I could go right to the campus for a visit and drop in for a chat. Boy that would be a surprise. I sometimes have fun with people I talk to and let them know which schools I've just sent papers to. I probably shouldn't do that, and I absolutely won't commit college names to print here. Just for laughs, I'll let on that these three students are at a large, public university on the West Coast. There. I've had a smile.*

All the barista here knows is that I have been writing about this one story for a good, long time. I've had a large, hardcover anthology lying next to the laptop held open to the right pages with a coffee cup sleeve and I've been up and down pacing and thinking for the past several hours. Perhaps hopefully, he looks across the counter at me and asks, "What'cha been working on all day?"

I show him the book and he asks which stories. When I tell him only one, he looks puzzled. "Long paper?"

Section I: Studies in Forgery

"No, just have to try it from a few different perspectives. Then I'll turn it in."

"Wow, that's a lot of work. Can't believe you are going to write it three times. You must be a perfectionist. Do you do this all the time?"

"Sometimes I do it four or five times," I shake my head.

"You're kidding! Man, I need your help some time—you could write one of my papers and help me pass this stupid English class."

Maybe, I think, but you're not getting a price break. I smile and give him a thumbs up and a wink. He's satisfied that we've connected on some sort of insider level. I can't help but laugh as I get back to the task at hand.

It's absolutely vital that I have three distinct writing voices and styles in this sort of circumstance. If I don't pay attention to this matter, it will cause problems for the clients, and then problems for me. Imagining having to do three revisions—all for free—is beyond thinking. Focus. I have come to calling myself "me, myself, and I" during these moments. I honestly don't know what I would call an additional persona if there were four papers to write instead of three. The overall task of writing three essays at more or less the same time is not difficult. It is just like any other day of writing for FraudPapers as schedules and deadlines overlap a bit. If I take a breather and have a few cups of coffee between papers, I'll speed right through. It helps, too, to keep the papers all open on the screen in front of me. Then I can make sure to occasionally do electronic word searches to make sure I'm not repeating phrasing and key words too often. Nice trick, isn't it? Professors do it all the time, and count on it too much of the time. Today's assignment is The Castle of Otranto *for a sophomore literature class. The professor wants his students to take one literary term, define it, look for it in the story, and write an essay about their findings. Well, three papers, then, each analyzing it from a different aspect. It's much easier to create and maintain completely disparate voices, structures, and nuances if I don't try to write the same paper for each one, so to speak. I've gone for essays addressing symbolism, theme, and, ironically, voice. Pretty easy, basic stuff. I can't even believe this is a sophomore level class. I've lost a bit of respect for the school, despite its solid reputation. Then again, it is a scientific school, as opposed to a liberal arts one. No need to worry about groundbreaking work in the English literature realm. I ensure that I've written what I call "fairway" papers. These are the safe essays. They cover exactly the topics professors expect in a basic fashion. Nothing dramatically good or over-the-top, and certainly nothing deficient. Right down the middle of the fairway, and stay away from the bunkers. I don't over swing, hit submit a few times, and I'm off and ready to enjoy a downtown stroll. Thank goodness for cheater networks.*

Seminar: The last few seminars discussed the primary groupings behind the academic forgery clientele. They provided insight into just what sort of students out there are supporting the habit, the business of cheating. There is another way to group and analyze the clients as a whole. It is the retail, or business model, view. Everything that can be said about academic forgery can be said about any other business in America. There is a product that is produced and sold wholesale, it is then shipped to retail outlets, and the customer buys it. With any luck for the company, two things will happen. First, the customer will be satisfied and continue to come back and buy more products. Second, the customer will tell others about his positive experience, and they will come and buy the product, too. Then this process will repeat exponentially over time. It is a combination of supply, demand, and experience. When all of these are in line with expectations, businesses thrive. That is the easiest way to understand academic forgery. It is not just a bunch of writers helping students to cheat. That's not it at all, actually. That is only what is being seen. What is unseen is the business aspect of forgery. Typical men and women on the street, even those who are less naïve and imagine that there are cheaters in colleges can't get themselves to really believe, really grasp the notion, that not only is this a common part of the campus experience, but that it extends far beyond that imagining. It isn't just cheating. It isn't just fraud. It is an established business, with competitors, leaders in the market, and those companies always on the cutting edge. It is just another sector of the American economy, and typifies it. The writers are factory level workers. They work in the mills, figuratively speaking, produce the papers which are the product in the inventory, and the product gets sent wholesale to the company. Then the company charges a marked-up retail rate to the consumers who are the students. The resulting revenue trickles down into wages for the original factory level operators. Write, retail, repeat. Simple as that. What is best is that there is little to no overhead expense incurred by neither the companies involved, nor their writers, who really aren't their employees at all. Further, because demand is so high, the prices continue to rise each year. Then the writers are paid a bit more. On and on it goes, and unemployed college graduates with writing skills see this as a career opportunity. They are even more convinced and better-financed when the market trends upward. This is especially true when two of three particular groups outperform marketing expectations.

The three categories explored initially were the liars, the legacies, and the losers. Again, though, this only expressed their personalities. But forgery doesn't depend upon these personalities as much as what they truly represent. They translate into three distinct business opportunities for forgers: honest cheats, career cheaters, and cheater networks. The most important to business needs for academic forgers are the latter two. When they grow, it is a bull market for fraud.

The honest cheats are where the liars are found. Calling them honest may be doing them a favor that is undeserved. These students are not marginal in nature, academically. There is rarely an indication in their orders that they are somehow deficient when it comes to their education. It really only comes down to either effort or circumstances, or maybe a combination of these elements. In any event, honest cheats sincerely believe that they will only use the service once. The second time they think that they will only use the service twice. That is usually the extent, actually, of their professional activities. What normally happens is that these average students run out of time—or sometimes patience—for a particular assignment. Usually this is a writing assignment, because the student's opinion is that writing takes a long time, especially if research is involved. If an essay's due date on a syllabus closes in on the student, he begins to panic. Some projects can be wrapped up quickly, and simple online quizzes can be taken on a short notice, but writing a whole paper from scratch? That is a scary thought to many a good pupil, even. It is easy to identify an honest cheat's order, and to distinguish it from others. The deadlines for these are usually very short. It is not out of the realm of common experience to see these orders pop up with fewer than three to four hours left before they have to be submitted. They are also almost always for online classes, and therefore the hour of the day for these to be turned in are the hours surrounding midnight, depending on the time zone of the writer. So, midnight, give or take three hours. That is, of course, if the student in question doesn't live somewhere like Australia. It happens. In addition, the special instructions and requests boxes are generally full of very nervous comments, because the clients have not used the services before. Even if they have heard through the grapevine that this sort of thing can get done, and done well, and meet the standards and expectations needed, the elements of stress and uncertainty accompany their order. Questions are downright silly sometimes. "Do you know MLA standards for citations? That's what I really need." Or, "I need a five paragraph essay structure, and it has to have one introductory paragraph, then three body paragraphs, and then a conclusion. Please make sure that you take the time to put good topic sentences at the beginning of each body paragraph, too." Please. It is easy to see that these clients are only trying to get something done quickly, and are a little bit out of their minds with stress and worry, having never done this before. It is somewhat like a blind dating site where fraud and forgers meet.

Needless to say, this is not one of the more important groups behind the business of academic forgery, or the bank accounts for academic forgers. The system would, in fact, run a lot smoother without the distractions of this slightly meddlesome group. Apart from the last-minute deadlines which result in additional premiums being charged, they don't make a large contribution to ongoing revenues. They almost never result in bonuses for writers, either, since these clients never stick around long enough to know about submitting writer reviews and the like. Again, they are not likely to return, either. These are dead-end clients. The liars dominate this group called the honest cheats.

Losers and legacies are grouped together for the purpose of supporting the business institutions called academic forgery companies, or paper mills. It's probable that the legacies themselves would be appalled at being called losers, but it is quite true. The main focus of both these types of individuals is that they want a lot of work done by other people. Academic forgers love the losers and legacies found in this combined grouping and have a name for them as a whole: career cheaters.

The name is appropriate in two ways. First is the more readily apparent one. The cheaters themselves make a career out of avoiding their own work. They do not intend to spend much of their academic life doing the petty little tasks that are called essays. It may be true that these clients do everything themselves when it comes to their major study, as well they should, but everything labeled general education requirement (which usually means writing essays) is pawned off on others. As pointed out earlier, there is no battle of ethics or moral tenets among these students. A metaphor that comes up when forgers consider these customers is of a person who owns a brand new sports car. They may do the washing of the car themselves, showing off the auto while waxing and buffing it. When it comes to actually changing the oil, however, well that more mundane task is usually left to the grease monkeys.

The nomenclature of career cheater is also apt when it comes to what the cheaters do for the careers of their writers. Even as they make a career out of not doing their own work, they make a career for the forger himself. Career cheaters like the certainty of having their own writer in their corner to whom they can come time and again for nearly anything that comes up. This is great for the writer. He appreciates the fact that he doesn't have to go looking for orders as much, and there is something that stokes the ego when a customer comes to you over and over, calling you his writer, or congratulating and lauding you for the results that you have brought to him over the days, weeks, months, years, etc. It's nice being on staff with a paid position, after all. The career cheater pays the forger's bills and keeps him in coffee each and every day he opens his laptop. In this fashion, a good career cheater doesn't even need to order expensive or difficult papers. In fact, it is probably better for the forger if he doesn't. It is easy to crank out four page essays on simple topics in a daily routine. There's not a lot of guesswork involved. It can't be overstated, and it will be stated many times in this book, that forgers do not like hassles. They like quick and easy. They like simple and dependable paychecks. Writing two papers for a total of forty-five dollars is far more preferable to writing one longer or complicated work for fifty dollars. The professional forger will always choose the former. The ironic fact of the matter is that he will probably write those two papers and have them delivered and the money in the bank before he would ever get that one paper done. And then there may be unpaid revision requests with the more difficult one. The typical career cheater provides many renditions of the simple payment plan for his personal forger.

If there is one misunderstanding among the American public regarding the whole affair of academic forgery, it is the perception that the first group, the honest cheats, makes up the bulk of what there is in the college cheating business. A common refrain is, "I'm sure it happens once in a while." Well, yes, for the liar or honest cheat, this is true. But the real business, the bulk of the thriving industry, comes from the career cheaters and one even more surprising sector—the cheater networks, as Ossi referred to in his case study above.

If there ever was a community of individuals called "friends with benefits" it would be the cheater networks involved in the pursuit of academic forgeries. These type of clients go well beyond the notions and behaviors of the career cheaters because it is not just for themselves and by themselves. It isn't comparable at all to someone who likes a writer and gives him everything to do. It is the supercenter model of the retail environment. To look at it in collegiate context, it is like one gigantic fraternity house. All it takes to be successful (both for the group and the forgers) is a little homogeneity. Here are two examples of how this bolsters academic forgery's position as an American business giant.

Certain clubs and organizations on well-known college campuses around the country are focused much more upon extra-curricular activities than their academic pursuits. Unless, that is, their pursuits involve chasing down forgery contacts. That is the advantage of belonging to a large, well-organized clique. There is usually a point person assigned to discover which forgers' houses produce consistent results. That means papers on time that are not discovered which could lead to a black eye for the university and suspensions for important individuals. It has little to do with money. These groups are very results-oriented. Once a few writers have been identified in a ghostwriter stable as being among the very best, they have all the business they can handle. Request after request come to them. All are sent with the specific writer's number and go directly to the writer's inbox. Almost always they are accompanied by a short message and a reasonable deadline. "Just like all the others, please," it may read. Given the fact that so many of these papers come in at about the same time, each with the same instructions and much of the same research suggestions, the idea that they have all circumstantially materialized is a farce. This is an example of a cheater network in action. What is most promising to forgers, and equally disturbing to the everyday American is the fact that these networks outlive any one class. It is not as if there is a four-year limitation to these activities. Once one senior class from this peer group graduates, the next class is right in line. As long as the contact person continues providing the information to the next batch of students, continuity exists. This belies what for many people is an uncomfortable but undeniable fact: the contact person is not a student. He is somehow connected to the university itself, as he connects successive graduating classes to their forgery setup. There is no other reasonable explanation for what is clearly going on. If a student were in charge, he would eventually graduate and leave the group. Then there would be a challenge with continuing to maintain the information necessary to pass on the success. The finding that year after year the students maintain academic eligibility for their extracurricular activities proves that there is some managing going on. The group keeps their status, the forgers keep their money and extend their writing careers. Many people on the street find this difficult to believe. Believe it—the forgers sure do.

The second example of a well-crafted network like this is organized around cultural grounds. This is an extension of the foreign factor. Instead of being students here and there who have fallen under the various pressures of parental or familial influences, this form of cheater network involves much more deliberate planning. Again, it works like a fraternity or club. At some point in an institution's history, certain students who were not native speakers of English came up with the idea of finding someone to help them with their composition papers. That interest then turned into finding paper mills to accommodate their needs. Then the cheaters found that some companies and writers were better than others and focused their efforts on a very specific, directed approach to these writers. As the cheaters approached graduation, their writers were still easily accessible. They weren't graduating or going anywhere. The next batch of students with this distinct national or cultural background—quite often relatives or members of a certain community— arrived to find that "help" was already arranged if necessary for these types of assignments. This alleviation of pressure at the onset of the collegiate experience allows for a smooth, careful transition to this next stage of life for the culturally-connected students in question.

As with the previous cheater network, this cohort is even more open about their connections to the forger. Almost every request begins with a semblance of, "I was recommended to you by a student you may have written for. His essay was about this certain subject and I would like it just like that, please." It is that polite, although not always as eloquently or concisely put. What is certain is that one forger who finds himself connected to a cheater network of foreigners can go for a long time without ever having to look for an order. All he has to do is be present, available, and willing. Every day orders will come in, and as he is collecting his money, the next set of orders follows. It is like clockwork, set to someone else's culturally-inclined clock. The only challenging thing that comes along with this specific group is the occasional difficulties with language. The forger has to have a particular set of skills to be able to write in a variety of qualities and accents. Each and every writer makes his own decision fairly early in his career whether or not to get involved with the foreign factor at all. It isn't for everybody.

This area of business is really where the money is when it comes to academic forgery in America. Without cheater networks, the industry would look quite different and be much less successful. It would also bring down many of the forgery houses. It is the cheater network cycle that plagues American academia today.

Without this conveyor belt operation of forgery requests which come every semester, year after year, forgery companies would have difficulty maintaining even, predictable revenue. Unlike other business sectors in America like tech companies, there really is nothing new that can be offered. That is actually good for the forgers, and enables them to succeed every day. It is the constant reliance on the classics of literature specifically that keep companies alive. This will not change anytime in the near future, as the system of academia has steadfastly relied upon teaching the classics for time out of mind. Even with the rise of the community colleges and business schools which are more career-focused and practical-minded, the numbers of students needing the "typical college paper" rarely changes, and has only grown over the past several decades. The ability of companies to garner the lion's share of these orders every academic term is the key to success, then. It is not about the next new thing, or the latest toy or gadget. The only thing that allows certain mills to stand apart and grow is their ability to create connections with groups, not individuals.

Beyond personal recommendation, there is just no really good way of marketing a forgery company's wares beyond simple search engine placement and results. Those results can be skipped or clicked on by will or whimsy. While a good personal recommendation can turn a client into a paycheck, a good cheater network recommendation maximizes the potential for thousands of paychecks. If the networks were to go down, the number of forgery orders would plummet. If the order totals decreased greatly but the numbers of companies didn't (at least right away), and the clients weren't being herded any one particular direction, their collective orders would spread and diffuse throughout the industry. It is easy to see where this is headed because the concept is so simple and straightforward. It is exactly like what happens in all other retail endeavors. Why the American public doesn't consider academic forgery to be a massive business operation that runs on the same concepts as do their local grocery store is difficult to fathom. So to conclude the preceding scenario, the spreading and diffusing of orders would water down each company's net business income. That would lower the opportunities and paychecks for the forgers themselves, as they begin to compete for a dwindling number of clients. Imagine, academic forgers being laid off. Companies would shrink and fail, and the overall numbers of outlets offering papers for purchase would diminish. It is not as if academic forgery would necessarily disappear altogether, as the honest cheats and career cheaters would still provide a reduced level of business, but the hydra would lose heads, for sure. The problem, in a nutshell, is that even honest cheats and career cheaters eventually graduate, move on, and leave their forger. Without a network to provide the next client, forgers would be left hoping for more lucky finds in the order queue.

This scenario of collapsing cheater networks, in fact, represents the American academic world's best chance at lessening the abilities of academic forgers to infiltrate and inundate universities and colleges with their papers. Rather than focusing schools' efforts on individual cheaters, which will always need to be done as a matter of course anyhow, the leaders of the ethics committees should strive to seek out the networks in their schools. These groups are offering the lifeblood to the bane of the forgery business. For each student that is discovered to have submitted fraudulently obtained papers, there is one more to catch. If he is not connected to any other cooperative seeking access to papers, if he is just a lone wolf type of cheater, the net result for the university is a plus-one rating. Then it is back to detective work, trying to find the next student to snare and punish. It is an exacting, difficult, and ultimately useless endeavor. The academic forgery world will not turn to chaos if honest cheats and career cheaters get taken out of the market. It is up to the schools to find out if they have cheater networks embedded on their campuses.

This is really common sense. It is not difficult at all, when pondered even momentarily, to identify possible areas in which the networks are operating. First of all, when a single forged paper is found, there should be an evaluation of the context of the fraud. Bringing the student in and slapping him on the wrist and sending him back will not do anything except perhaps keep him from trying it again. What if the university took their time on the matter, however? If they immediately suspended the student and investigated things a bit more thoroughly, they could determine if there was a pattern that could be deciphered. Does the student belong to a group that looks like a cohort system? Are forgeries being found coming from students who belong to certain peer groups, types of students, nationalities, or extra-curricular activities? Are certain ESL student organizations showing high rates of forged paper submissions? All of these findings could be made and catalogued. If done well, and thoroughly, and above all patiently, post-secondary education institutions across the United States could begin to whittle down the academic forgery market by going after cheater networks.

5

The Double Blind

The Forger at Work: *When I first found FraudPapers I was not going to be rejected. Again, the writer's ego at play. If I got turned down as an essay writer with my credentials, it would have been a crushing blow. Therefore, I sent the company an inundation of writing samples and a hefty* curriculum vitae. *Without knowing it, I was already becoming familiar with the forger's art. I created a perception of myself for the company to see. As time goes by, I am not only honing my writing skills, but my skills at showing only the side of myself that I want to be known for. I am becoming Ossi Chesterton, Academic Forger.*

My initial research into FraudPapers aroused some interesting observations. A web search of the company's name confirmed some of my suspicions. Straight off, my concerns were whether or not the business was real, or just a typical online scam. It is an indictment of my moral condition, I suppose, that my worries that forgery may not be the most honest of professions was quite secondary to the desires of being employed as a writer. Some rather unsettling news popped up on my monitor. There were many forums and blogs dedicated to complaints about the company itself. These ranged from writers claiming non-payment issues, to writers being improperly charged by the company for plagiarizing their work. Considering that I wanted to be one of those writers very soon, I was growing worried. All issues with moral righteousness aside, I didn't want to be entering into a business that may not reliably pay me or accuse me of not writing properly. It was definitely worth checking into. Was FraudPapers a legitimate opportunity for me, or was it just as scandal-ridden for the writers as it was for the customers and the schools they attend? This was a good chance to use my research skills. Who exactly were these people who were dragging the good name of the forgery company through the mud? Did they truly have an ax to grind?

5. The Double Blind

Nearly all of the complaints came from individuals who were allegedly rejected or dismissed by FraudPapers. They flunked out at helping students cheat. Some of them wrote a paper or two and then were let go or got fined by FraudPapers for failing to follow policies and procedures. Others wrote that they submitted absolutely great work and then were fired for supposedly cutting and pasting the work from research sites, or even from other essay writing sites. Even more were fighting, they stated, to get their proper payments from the company. Was this something that I wanted to get involved with? Then again, though, there was a common thread that ran through all of these blog entries. From reading their pleadings and bickerings, it was apparent that the writers in question did not seem like the best-of-the-best that I encountered during my time in college. Some of them wrote their statements poorly, even. If this was an example of their work, then they probably were dismissed for cause. Remember the writer's ego? I assumed that these guys weren't nearly as good as they claimed, and that they washed out of the business. Now they were mad. That made sense. No worries, then ... I'm quality. The most intriguing of posts I found assured readers that a sinister rumor that was spreading was true: FraudPapers secretly owns much of the competition and operates as a shell business. It did seem like there was a shroud of secrecy surrounding the field of academic forgery. Yet the mystery itself was somewhat exciting. I joined anyway.

That mystery grew once I began working in earnest. Sure enough, there were numerous policies and procedures that every writer with FraudPapers needed to commit to. They were simple. No plagiarizing. No lying about sources used. Submit assignments on time. Do not arrange for payments outside of the normal company/client exchange. It was a standard business contract. In fact, it was like starting a job anywhere else. You get hired and the first thing that is done is an orientation where the manager talks a bit and hands you an oversized packet of new hire information. So it wasn't particularly sinister and alleviated some of my worries. A few minutes into my reading I did find some interesting tidbits. I was instructed to not share any personal information with my clients. Absolutely nothing at all. I had to ensure that my name was not used anywhere in my work or correspondence with clients. I was never to discuss my education (I later found out that sometimes the company embellishes the writer's credentials, so best not to divulge something that may be contradictory), or share writing samples with them. We, the customers and I, were not to know each other's time zones, even! The only way we were to communicate was through the company's messaging systems, and FraudPapers made it clear that they reviewed all of those messages. It was a system policy. I had entered the shadow world of pay-for-essay employment. And I liked it.

Seminar: It is not surprising at all to find out that there is a dense fog of information, and especially misinformation, surrounding academic forgery outlets. Despite the fact that the businesses are not violating any established laws, it is certain that they do not want to be undone by those possessing too much "dirt" on them. As I found out while working for FraudPapers, this low-grade paranoia extended not only to keeping clients in the dark, but keeping the writers uninformed, too. This overall secrecy can be broken down into three distinct parts. The first is clientele information; the second, writer information; the third, company information. Collectively, this is known as the double blind of academic forgery.

When it comes to the student who is attempting to purchase an essay online, it is obvious why he would not want to share his own information. Whether a liar, a legacy, or a loser, no one really wants to get caught cheating. Though there is no prohibition or penalty for the customer who divulges their personal details, the smart pupil knows to avoid this.

This is especially true when it comes to the first piece of the puzzle: the student's name. If this were to be recorded and later distributed for any reason, it could come back to haunt the person throughout his entire life. Is this dramatic, or actually realistic? Consider the timeline of the implications. To begin with, if his name is revealed to the school that he attends currently, the result could be immediate and serious. Every student across America, to the best of my knowledge, has to acknowledge the presence, and agree to it, of an academic conduct statement. This is variously known as the academic integrity standard, or academic standards statements, etc. It states mostly consistent versions of what constitutes cheating at the school, and the punishments surrounding violations of those circumstances. Usually, this centers on plagiarism, and although the consequences include probation, suspension and/or expulsion, generally it is the former which is actually enforced. Then there is the rather vague understanding of plagiarism that is implicit in the wording of these statements. Most students' concept of plagiarism is that it is merely using another source's exact words or very close paraphrasing without citing the source or otherwise attributing it clearly. What about actually using another person's entire paper? This is not covered on its face. It seems like it should be, but then again, seems is not the word upon which a contract is made.

Then again, there is the fact that most academic forgery papers contain no overt plagiarism beyond the fact that the paper is fraudulently turned in by the customer. Careful forgers who do not want dissatisfied clients or bosses accurately cite all sources used. They are well versed in the differing styles and methods of citations from basic MLA and APA all the way down to ASA (infrequently requested, but most forgers cover their bases pretty well). It is easy for the pupil to print the paper and turn it in, firmly believing that they are not plagiarizing at all. Everything will check out if the professor is keen on proving sources. This is truly some mental compartmentalizing that is going on here! No plagiarism, no problem. Thus thinks the student on the purchasing end of things. The academic integrity promise didn't specifically state that one shouldn't purchase a paper. Even though it would appear to be common sense, it is equally true that common sense does not a contract make.

When a student's name is revealed, there are indeed further complications that may come up. If the person in question manages to graduate from his undergraduate program without being detected, there are two other possibilities of things being ruined for him. To begin with, an application for graduate school may be in order (perhaps the word "order" shouldn't be attached to this thought). Graduate programs should be much more thorough in their efforts to prove applicants' abilities and backgrounds. They are more selective, after all. In addition, they brook no controversy when it comes to their schools. The one thing that would cause serious problems for the departments involved would be for research to be faked or worse, bought. The thought that a graduate student's name could be attached to a forgery scandal is unacceptable and would forever bar that student from getting in to an advanced degree program. That is what could happen. It is an indelible black mark. Not only would the student not get into his first choice of programs, but that restriction could easily follow him to every school to which he applies.

The publicity would make him infamous, and no academic institution wants the word infamous to be associated with them. Then there is an even more significant problem with the student's name being attached to academic forgery.

Presumably, if the student did graduate with his degree and is able to translate that accomplishment into gaining a job in the field *as a result of holding that qualification*, then what would happen to his career if it was later proven that he forged his coursework in the process of earning that degree? Wouldn't that be problematic? Most assuredly.

It is common knowledge that unemployment has been a serious concern for the past decade. Not only is this true of the blue-collar worker, but even more so for those who are pursuing career paths that are opened through the possession of an undergraduate degree. As pointed out earlier, this is especially true of those who graduated from liberal arts studies. If it wasn't difficult enough to break into a field in this arena, how much more so if it turned out that the degree was paid for to begin with? Consider someone who is looking to work in library science for a living, for example. There are a limited number of those positions, because there are a finite number of libraries, even counting private, public, and graduate facilities. This makes the competition for these spots intense. One has to be among the highest-pedigreed to successfully earn an opening. And if a connection with academic forgery is discovered, or even a charge levied? No hope. That dream of working in the field is over.

Though not as likely, this dilemma also can follow the student into work that is not in his own field. If he were to be precluded from library employment, then there must have been a discoverable means of showing this less-than-honorable character trait or history. Can other white-collar employers find this out, as well? Definitely. The information age ensures this. More and more frequently, hiring managers and human resources departments are looking to the Internet for background information on potential employees. Sometimes what comes up is entertaining, though no less damaging than findings on forgery. Photos posted on social websites of the candidate engaging in drunken binge parties (or worse) can and have been used to weed out the finalists for a job. Search engines can turn up information beyond just pictures. As much as employers would hope to type in the applicant's name and come up with results showing qualifications and accomplishments, they would be aghast if connections to academic misconduct such as forgery complaints were to be displayed. That would just about end the interview process. Hiring managers don't have time, or patience, to call the person back into another meeting and have him explain just why this had been returned on a search. There are enough other avenues of discussion in a positive sense that will return interviewees to the second or third level of meetings. The "don't call us, we'll call you" imperative is followed in this circumstance. So the would-be library scientist has now managed to wash out of his first choice of employment and subsequent choices, as well. Therefore, to backtrack, it is a damning condition that can be avoided through the secrecy of academic forgery in the first place. Careful clients are just that—clients, not names.

Writer information secrecy is the second consideration of life within the double blind. This is where things become a little strange. It is clear why the clients' information needs to be protected by them. But why should writers—or the companies that employ them—worry about this?

On its face, there is no reason. If a university stared down a student at the institution and made him confess (which, as it will be described later, is the only foolproof method), and if for whatever reason the name of the forger were divulged, so what? There is no recourse available to the school, or anyone else, for that matter. At the very worst, one very specific avenue of money would dry up for the writer. The only problem for him would be if the student used him as his personal writer. In that case, the forger loses his easily counted earnings and has to look to the order queue to make up for that, for a little while. If he is good enough to have dedicated clients, it is most likely that he will just pick up another one soon enough. No big deal.

That is the only challenge facing forgers when it comes to preserving their identification. There are simply no other complications. On a very pragmatic level, ironically, there is the integrity statement of the company for which he works. He pledged when taking the job that he wouldn't share his name or other information with the clients, and if this is discovered, then he will most likely lose his job. Now that is a bit ironic, forgers having to sign standards of behavior agreements. On an extended level, and this is somewhat far-fetched, a writer faces the same sort of career blackballing that a student does if his name becomes associated with academic forgery. All writers want to write for a living. Most of them do not want to do this through working for a paper mill. Therefore, these same writers are usually on the lookout for a "real" writing job. These would potentially include writing for a paper or magazine, copywriting positions, and the like. If, during the interview process, the words "academic forger" came up, then that would about end the application. The reason why this is an unlikely scenario is that the typical academic forger has already gone through numerous job searches before landing in their current assignments. They are usually frustrated former academics who thought they would be "real" writers or authors at this point in their lives. Forgery has become their inn of last resort. They are stuck and no longer worry about what this activity might mean for their futures.

Then there are the forgers who emotionally enjoy the excitement and intrigue of becoming the mystery authors behind international academics. They are the ones who consider themselves the true ghostwriters of the globe. Most of them no longer even use their own names when it comes to thinking about themselves as writers, anyway. Ossi Chesterton is one of them. The concept of having a nom de plume in the avenue is fantastical and fun. It offers something better than credibility, it offers daring. So the alias becomes their alter ego. Same with the writer's identification number. It is another way of participating in this world of make believe. Yes, many academic forgers either actually learn to love what they do and consider themselves better than the rest and above the academic world, or they at least convince themselves of that. Maybe that is actually more important. It helps them to not think about how they are failing to make a living in a respectable job.

Company secrecy is even stranger yet. This component of the double blind, or triple blind, or even more, makes no real sense. One would think that since the business of academic forgery is a retail operation like any other, that openness, especially when it comes to reputation and marketing, would be paramount. Secrecy would work against that aim. However, that couldn't be farther from the truth. Let's take a look at FraudPapers.

There are two ways to attempt to find information about a company like this. To begin with, consider just what a student can learn when seeking out a paper mill to go to for his first essay. After an exhaustive web search, he settles on the organization in question and clicks on the hyperlink. Here is what he finds.[1]

The home page indicates that it is a U.S. based business. That right there says something about what is going on when it comes to essay writing. Many of the companies are overseas, or at least claim to be. Nothing can be assured. This one, though, says that it is American. However, clicking on the "Contact Us" link does not lead to a physical address. Instead, an electronic form appears and instructs the customer to send questions in that way. Going back to the "About Us" link again only reveals the American status. The "Frequently Asked Questions" page only addresses the issue by restating that the writers are all U.S. based. And yes, the phone number is a toll-free one, yielding no area code information. With enough perseverance, and a bit of luck, hovering over a link on the ordering page opens up a dialog box with a phone number for contacting the company during the period in which the paper is being written. It is, indeed, a U.S. area code. There is also an e-mail address listed in this hidden box so that paying customers can contact the company directly. It is not, however, an address that reflects the company's name. It is a completely different business entity, seemingly. If the name of the organization on the website is "FraudPapers," for example, the e-mail address is not FraudPapers.com or something like that. This is probably what leads some people to believe that there is a connection between varying academic forgery outlets. Are there really some larger groups behind the differing storefronts? It would appear so.

If the person trying to get information about the company takes the apparently real telephone number and runs it into a reverse phone number lookup engine, it returns a business name that matches the hidden e-mail address. Clicking on the business name provides a physical address, and yes it is in the proper area code in the United States. Ironically, this result comes up on a page populated by "featured business results" that include very well-known and respected national tutoring services. They probably wouldn't be happy with this arrangement. So why, if someone could go through these steps and finally determine exactly where the business is, does the company not just put this information right on the website? That is the strange part. But it gets decidedly stranger from here. When said prospective client cuts and pastes the name of this company that is shown in the reverse lookup and enters it into a search bar, there are two problems. First, the name closely matches a legitimate business that is not in the business of writing essays. Second, there is another search result for an essay-writing service that, when clicked on, takes the searcher to a company site that is not Fraud-Papers at all. It is another website for another essay writing service that has a completely different company name and contact information. This one's home page has testimonials from all over the globe splashed on it. Yet it has the exact same phone number in the United States. Same area code, same exchange, and everything. So it leads right back to the company name from the very first search.

As if this isn't interesting enough, taking a look at the bottom of the second company's home page, right after all of the testimonials, is a disclaimer. It describes plagiarism as being a crime and claims that their papers are only intended as models to be consulted. Yet, when backtracked to the original company's site, there is no disclaimer like this, and it is more than apparent that the papers are going to be submitted by clients. Remember the order box? Customers even request a specific range of numbers of words to be written for the essay. And this is so it could be an "example" of what to do? Right. So why all of the shell-game work going on here? There doesn't seem to be any rational reason for why a company, whether FraudPapers or whatever it may really be called, goes through all of this to scramble their information. It gets more and more intriguing the more one digs.

Working for the company provides even more data that doesn't make sense. One would think that the writer, who is ostensibly both a freelance writer and works for the company at the same time, would be able to have a more firm grasp of who is behind the enterprise. That, though, is as far from the truth as any of the above.

When I first encountered FraudPapers and they accepted me as one of their writers, I quickly learned that I wouldn't learn about them. Everything was automated. After the initial e-mail confirming that I was accepted, I was directed to the online environment for the writers. It included such things as how to set up my account for payment, how to check the database for orders, how to check my company e-mail and alerts, and that was about it. If I had a question about a specific order, whether while I was working on it, or simply thinking about taking it, there was no personal e-mail contact to whom I could direct my inquiry. Rather, there was a link to "order questions." When the answer came back, it came from the "no-reply" address, and was not signed off by anyone. There also wasn't any telephone number for writers to call into for questions or problems. Just the generic e-mail links. When writers submit the order for completion, there is simply a check box that indicates that the order is completed and that payment will be forthcoming. Indeed, the payment appears shortly thereafter in the bank account of your choice. That is all there is to it. A faceless, nameless organization. For mystery story fans, though, there is more....

After working for the company for a few months, I was promoted. My new status was that of Senior Writer. Apparently the combination of enough clients requesting my writer ID along with favorable reviews led FraudPapers to believe that I could be of more assistance to them if I were to take on more important assignments. To the company, that meant orders that were more expensive. These would include lengthier works, such as 40-plus page essays, and more complex assignments such as theses. Along with this change in rank came a guaranteed per-page rate that greatly exceeded what I had been working for, and other bonuses along the way. One thing the company made a big deal out of was the fact that I now had my own personal account manager. I had an actual person to turn to. She had a name, and an e-mail address. I could reach her. And, it turned out, she could reach me, too. At that point, I fully realized that all is not as it seems in the shadowy world of academic forgery.

I had become important enough to my manager to be held accountable at a moment's notice. This woman introduced herself to me in an e-mail and signed off with a very stereotypical, almost laughably cliché American name. I will let the reader come up with whatever variation he will choose to represent this. Then she called me one night with an urgent request. To begin with, it should be pointed out that the call came at 3:15 a.m. Eastern Standard Time. I had just gone to sleep an hour before that. When I checked the caller ID, it simply said "Service." To this day I don't know how that prompted me to actually pick up the call. I said hello, and the woman said she was my account manager, and introduced herself by name. I almost couldn't understand her, and it wasn't because of the time. It was her accent. She was not from this country, and her name could not have been what she claimed it was. No way. Also indicative of the fact that all was not what it seemed was the background noise from the caller's location. There were clearly many conversations in the background, all of them upbeat and chipper, and there is no believing that it was anywhere near three in the morning wherever these people were. It sounded much more like the middle of the business day. Once my account manager's words made it through the translator in my mind, I heard, "I am about order calling you. I am needing for client now a paper for your specializing." She told me to look in my inbox immediately and that I would find a very high-dollar order that had a lightning fast deadline on it. She trusted that I could get this done to her and the client's satisfaction. Then she hung up.

That was all.

After I shook the sleep from my eyes and turned on my computer, there it was: the exact assignment that my account manager had just described to me in so many, broken words. I looked again at my telephone. It did show that "Services" had just called. The account manager, she with the very Anglo-sounding name, was someone I would probably instead place somewhere right of Western Europe on a globe. Just for fun, I dialed up the number on my phone. "Services" was not a working number. It was the telephonic version of the "donotreply" e-mail address, after all.

That is how company information remains secret in the academic forgery world. For reasons unknown, the businesses are even more secretive than are any of the clients or the writers themselves. Despite all of the reasons that the latter two groups would want to maintain their confidentiality, the same can't really be said about the essay-writing services. They make their money by students finding them and by ordering essays. It doesn't seem like they would necessarily want to hide. By legal statute, what they are doing is not illegal. Unethical, yes. Damaging to the students' academic and perhaps occupational careers? Of course. Yet, they seem to attempt to hide even more than anyone they provide their products to. They still rake in the cash, though.

That reaffirms the fact that marketing to first-timers isn't where the money is. The cheater networks take care of all of that for companies like FraudPapers. Like one of the testimonials eloquently stated on its splash page exudes: "I love you guys, and I'm telling all of my friends!"

6

Competitors and Honorable Forgery

The Forger at Work: *My reputation is growing. Now the company itself is directing work straight to me. If it was nice having a growing stable of my own clients who depend upon me on a routine basis, it is even more flattering to be on the receiving end of these orders. I just got a message from my account manager that I would be getting an order that represents an initial contact for the company. She, my manager, would like to use me to take on orders from first-time customers in order to pull them into the fold long term. Hopefully, too, she continues, customers who had problems with other essay writing companies could be provided top-notch papers by me as one of FraudPapers' senior writers, and then would come to us as a repeat user. Maybe user isn't quite the right word, with all of its connotations, but at the same time it seems apt. I am sure there is a "hint, hint" implicit in the message that my manager sent me. Something like, maybe this customer will want to support you personally in the future, right? I don't need to be told twice. Here's the message now.*

The contact form in front of me comes from a very frustrated, and yet hopeful, customer. He lets me know that he is really counting on me, because he has had such bad experiences in the past with other companies. Apparently he dealt with two different operations who sent him pre-canned papers. He browsed, clicked, and paid. They weren't as good as he thought they would be, which is probably why he isn't a professor. The papers he turned in sure didn't fool the real deal. Imagine that. Now he is trying out FraudPapers. When he called, yes apparently he managed to call us, he was one exasperated fellow. After a little talking back and forth, the manager assured him he would have the personal attention of one of the best writers they had (their words, not mine). All the customer had to do was provide the particulars, and voilà, it would be sent directly to the writer of choice. It was in my box, electronically speaking, within ten minutes.

So the phrasing was like this: "Dear Writer, I've tried this whole thing out before and can't even believe I'm doing it again. Two other companies got me caught and almost thrown out of school. I can't afford to have this happen. The person I talked to said they'd send me to the right person for the job, and I sure hope he wasn't giving me a bunch of b.s. Like I said, I've been down this road before, you know? It's not even that big of a deal. I'm going to give you one paper for you to show me you're for real and then if it's all good, I've got two more that need to be redone."

A few thoughts are already crossing my mind as I'm reading through this rather plaintive wail/rant. First, he had two other companies almost cause him to be expelled? Not only is this a ludicrous way to look at things, but wow, there is some lack of common sense going on in this guy's head. He is a real believer in the adage "third time's a charm." I have to admit I almost want to be the one to push him right over the academic edge, which doesn't speak well for the attitude that we forgers can get from time to time. How dare he buy a paper, have it go wrong, and then turn around and blame the forger's company? Another blip on my radar got my hackles up right away. Clearly this student is not a good judge of who will do a proper writing job for him, as his past experiences show, but he says he is going to "give me one chance?" Because he is the expert? I should calm down. He is going to pay for today's coffee, at least. Maybe more if I meet his expectations. Then again, he is probably paying a pretty penny since he went the route of describing his painful circumstances and exacting needs to one of the account reps. That whole line about making sure he'll get the right person to help him? Translated, that means that the student will be charged more, and somehow this premium will make him feel more secure about his purchase. Retail, right? I dare anyone to tell me they didn't at least once buy a more expensive product because they felt more confident in the name brand. Same with forgeries. It just wouldn't inspire the student's confidence if he were turning in a paper thinking, yeah, here's the cut-rate copy. Please give me a great grade! I scroll up the order page. There it is, the little icon that indicates a high-value paper. I didn't even think to look first time around. I should have known. Then again, because the company sent this one to me directly, I guess I did know, and so never considered having to check it out.

I don't have much going on at the moment, and so decide to take a little time with this client. I would love for him to be a regular, so I'll give him some extra personal attention. Time to put a bit of charm and effort into it. I e-mail him before even beginning the work. "Dear client, Thank you for contacting me about your order. I'm sure you've been frustrated by your past experiences, and I'd like to know more about what caused your problems. Let me know what went wrong with the papers you've gotten from those other companies. The more I know, the more I'll be able to take care of you." I'm so nice, aren't I? Yeah, the more I know, the more I'll be able to take care of you ... or the more I know, the more I'll be able to get you hooked on my paper writing.

I should be a used car salesman.

Seminar: By now, it shouldn't surprise readers that the above situation exists. There are so many students cheating and so many different operations supporting their efforts, not to mention taking their money, that variations upon typical retail experiences occur every day. The only real difference between what is going on in this quasi-academic environment and the local big-box stores is how customer service is handled.

There is not a whole lot of recourse available to the student who purchases papers from online mills. It is pretty much a one-time shot in the dark, per paper. Many, if not most, institutions at the college level do not afford their students the opportunity to revise and resubmit work. This is especially true of large universities where a single professor with perhaps one or two teaching assistants has to grade hundreds of papers per week. The grade given is, quite frankly, the grade of record. Community colleges and smaller, private schools often have more leeway to allow a second go at things for their pupils, which ironically could lead to more cheating. That is an interesting conundrum.

Where the large scale schools, and presumably the large-scale cheating, are considered, the money is really on the line for the liars, legacies, and losers. Typically, the more active and experienced group, the losers, understand that they need to get the most for their money and have already used a "reliable" or "reputable" source to which they continue to return. As a result, this seminar doesn't wholly apply to that category. The other two, however, run into these problems with alarming frequency. They simply do not know better, and with the rise of inexpensive and flashy websites, they get the wool pulled right over their eyes. This is a great social experiment in the successes of marketing, by the way. If someone in the market for a product is particularly needy and pressed for time, they are much more likely to be drawn into a company's lot (to use an auto sales metaphor) by the rotating search lights and brightly colored neon signs. That's the same with the essay-writing sites. When clicked on, these home pages are usually multi-color affairs, with flashy, and sometimes flashing, text boxes and easy-to-find hyperlinks leading to the order page. The progression of online journalism—like gossip columns and sports pages—shows itself in the search results that directed the buyers in the first place. You know the type.

Blurbs like "Shocking papers fool even the best professors," "One easy way to cheat in college," and "A papers for CHEAP" are just enough hyperbolic text to garner a quick peak. Students in a hurry can't help themselves when it comes to these claims. When the search yields a longer amount of dry wording such as, "Our services have five years of experience behind them, providing academic papers in a variety of subjects…" that just isn't exciting or fast enough to take in the last-minute plea. It just sounds like too much work, ironically enough, and smacks of deadlines not being met. So there are clearly many competitors out there in the academic forgery market, each offering their wares in varying fashion, using different marketing. Some sell quality, some sell cheap, and even more post the wording "quality and cheap" on the websites. What, if anything, differentiates them?

The concepts of competitors and honorable forgery really do go hand in hand. The cliché regarding honor among thieves does apply, I have found. It is not that the upstanding companies are morally upright, of course, but they at least do provide a superior product. This seminar will explore two of the myriad choices available to a typical liar customer who is looking for that one, special paper. He begins by typing in the memorable words, "buy an essay."

The first company he chooses from the results looks professional. It doesn't contain all caps in its description, and uses complete sentences rather than short, exciting blurbs. This looks good, he thinks, and proceeds to their page. Sure enough, it does look good. The site uses professional-looking fonts and is set up much like a college paper outline, to boot. Each section is in bold, with indented supporting claims. The picture at the top is a nice, nearly sepia-toned textbook with a fountain pen. The buyer's confidence is growing. A free consultation chat box even opens, off to the side where it doesn't occlude the text. What about its guarantees? Customized papers, individual advice, no plagiarism, and protection of privacy. What really stands out is that the no plagiarism promise is the first thing listed. Sounds like a winner. Furthermore (the company actually uses the word "moreover" which is a professional, polysyllabic touch) they provide a free first draft, free outlines, free bibliographies, and free delivery. This is representative of an honorable forgery outlet, for reasons that will be described below.

The second company, however, is vastly different. It is exciting! The homepage has flashing, sliding banners. Each slide reveals a beautiful young girl with a huge smile, usually giving a thumbs-up or an O.K. sign. There are numerous testimonials, such as, "Your writing is a very great!" Yes, the company used a testimonial that is not grammatically correct. The claims on this site include affordable, money-back guarantees, and discounts. I'm sure they also mean quality, but it doesn't appear to be a priority. The word plagiarism only appears once, in small print, well down the page. And even better, there is a database of papers to choose from if you can't wait for a customized essay! There are even unlimited revisions offered. Presumably, the business is not stating that they may not get it right the first time, or even the second or third time. This is representative of the not-so-honorable competitor in the essay writing business.

What really stands out when looking at these two services, all flashiness aside, is the fact that one provides only customized works, and one offers a wide variety of pre-written essays to choose from if the client is in a hurry. It is a good thing for students who choose the latter option that there are so many paper mills in operation. If said student needs a paper on the villainy of Iago (a personal favorite of mine), and he scans the existing papers until he finds one that just looks perfect, the chances are that many other like-minded students have also found this particular paper to be just right in its appearance and topical coverage. How many identical essays are then being turned in around the country? It is difficult to tell, as that sort of statistic is never provided. It would be counterintuitive for the company to flash in big, bright script, "Our most successful essay ever! It's been turned in to classes 10,000 times!" Even students who aren't quite as bright as the flashing icon could presumably know that he may not want to turn in essay number 10,001 and get caught. The sheer prevalence of the paper on the academic market would seem to exponentially increase the chances of it being discovered. Then again, the company, and the student, are both counting on the fact that there are just so many collegiate institutions, sections, and professors, that this chance will remain minute. And they're right, by and large. I have never talked to a professor who did, in fact, have two identical papers turned in to him, even over the course of several semesters. So the businesses stay in business.

The honorable competitor does not offer pre-written papers. It doesn't even show examples of essays on its site, which prevents anyone from simply cutting and pasting. It makes good use of the words "unique," "qualified," and "authentic" to hawk its papers. These are good words to see, and help to settle the nerves of first-time buyers. This is a company like FraudPapers. Each and every essay ordered and purchased on the site is hand-crafted by a writer who writes it from scratch, with the thesis provided by the customer, using the sources that the customer asks for (if available), and in the exact length and format requested. When done well, these fakes are undiscoverable. It is truly as if the student himself wrote it. The only possible thing that could trip up the client is if some-how the professor intuitively knows that the writing is too high of quality to match the student's ability. That is highly unlikely in today's academic world. Since the writer from the stable uses his sources judiciously and cites appropriately, again in the style that is needed, there is also no chance of it being found out by anti-plagiarism software that is utilized by many instructors. The number of hits will be low, and each hit will be shown to be well-cited upon review. Hence, the claim of quality, individualized papers from the company. They are right. These assignments, for which the student will pay more money, will deliver every time.

This disparity between outlets shows itself in many other ways, too. The fast-and-easy route should be warning enough to would-be buyers, but it appeals to their current needs. This is quite true of the last-minute effort typically found with the honest cheats. But there should be a caveat attached to these sites, to be fair. Whereas the honorable ones give every-thing that is necessary for a completed paper that will not be rejected by a professor, the less-than-honorable skimp, usually because of short deadlines. Sometimes bibliographies are not done. The sources may be shown on a separate page, but nothing is formatted—that is up to the student. Often, there is no title page, or an outline is asked for by the professor but the student doesn't get one with his order. If the student is really in a hurry, he has no chance to get this done by himself. The result will be a bad grade, at best, or a completed failed paper, at worst. And that money-back guarantee? Good luck. Has anyone ever heard of a forgery mill being turned in to the Better Business Bureau? Typically the BBB only responds to complaints involving a specific location for a business, not just some vague online address. And I have never seen the phrase "Better Business Bureau approved" on an essay-buying site.

By contrast, the honorable company ensures that the work is complete. From title or cover page to endnotes and bibliographies, it will fit the bill, so to speak. Headers and footers are all appropriate, and citations are specific. Concerning citations, too, the phrase "consider the source" comes into play here as a distinction. Time and again, students are made aware that certain online "research" sites are not approved for academic writing. They are either too broad, and therefore not truly educational, or they are not properly researched. Any contributor who believes that he is knowledgeable can post their "findings" which are merely opinions onto the site. Then these opinions are distributed and accepted as fact by users of the site. Unfortunately for the students who then tack these into their papers, the bibliography is revelatory, and rejected. Yet the less-than-honorable essay writing companies have been known to sell papers that utilize these sources. Even where they are properly notated, they are still improper as a whole and the paper will be failed. Now that is an iron-clad guarantee.

Then there are the various ways in which academically approved sources are used. Whereas the better outlets support their arguments with economical research, prudently applied, the others do the opposite. They cut and paste large chunks of research findings and then support those blocks with a few lines of text. This leads, as one can guess, to two distinct problems: first, the professor is looking for a student's writing and original work, not just regurgitation of others' and secondly, if not properly cited the entirety will come back as a huge product of plagiarism. Either way, the student is doomed. The companies that supplied this inferior product don't care. If the student complains, they will usually get ignored. Their disgust will never be posted as a testimonial. What if they post something online as an isolated, negative review? Students I've talked with never take those reviews seriously. There is a double standard involved here. The students who are about to cheat somehow consider themselves to be above those who have fallen prey to ruses. So they ignore those posts.

Basically, this all leads to much of the business eventually being routed to the slightly more expensive academic forgery outlets that provide a superior product and experience. Unfortunately for the writers of those businesses, their first contacts with these customers is difficult, challenging, and sometimes highly emotionally charged. In the forger's case study, one example of that is shown. "Two other companies got me caught," is what the buyer stated. Most likely, the customer got tied into an essay writer who used significant cutting and pasting. Hence the use of the word "caught." It wasn't as if he complained about his papers being improper, or too short, or missing pieces, or even about being poor quality. All of these things may have been true, as well, but his chief concern was that he got caught. Plagiarism was probably the culprit. The client didn't indicate whether he bought an essay that was readily available on the site, or if he had an actual writer that did him in. Either way, he has now gotten to FraudPapers and is mad. So the writer has to deal with this issue. The quality and product will not be a problem for the forger. What is problematic is getting over the hump with the student. He will probably be difficult to work with and hesitant to just accept what is given to him. Also, because he has already turned in the paper and it was rejected, he knows that there is something even more serious that has to be addressed. The instructor has seen the work and expects it to be revised. A completely rewritten paper with a different thesis and altogether different research will never work. The professor will notice that right away. Then he will ask those painful questions like, "Wow—you're a completely different writer on this one. Way to go! How did you have time to find all that new research in just a few days? What made you change your entire thinking about how to approach the topic? Why didn't you do this the first time around?" Or what if he challenges the student this way: "all right, student, I'm going to put this paper on my desk face down. Now why don't you explain to me what you wrote?" Oh no. There is no way the student has really absorbed the paper. He hasn't grappled with it in his own mind. He may not even know what the essay is about, or what its major points are. He is in significant trouble. If the student anticipates this, he then passes the problem on to the new writer of the reputable company.

This makes the good forgers very angry, and many of them won't get involved at all. First of all, these are the better writers who know they are truly better writers. They don't want to become associated with any hack's work. It is beneath them. The thought of having to take this thing called an essay and rework it ever so slightly to create quality is revolting. Yet that is what is necessary. The student is mad at the previous writer's work, but knows that a revision, not a complete rewrite, is in order. The inane comments are found in the order box, or in subsequent follow-up e-mails. "I needed MLA, not APA style. The citations are wrong. There is not enough writing and too many sources. And the sources aren't acceptable to my professor! I need this all changed. But don't make it obvious!"

So this writer, who knows better anyway, is getting yelled at for writing he didn't even do in the first place. Strangely enough, the reason he is involved at all is because he is such a good writer. The company that is trying to encourage the student to use its services full time knows that they had better hook the disgruntled client up with one of the senior staff writers in order to impress him. Then the customer will come back again, transforming him from liar to loser in the process. Hopefully, that loser will tell others and a new cheater network will be created. This is all on the shoulders of one of their top writers, who has to deal with this whole thing. Fortunately for him, he is paid more for every assignment because of his status. He has earned the right to be annoyed and pestered by these sorts of people. They are the sideshow attraction that surrounds his general work for regulars that support his pay. But he can't turn these down, usually. That will upset his account manager, who will threaten his status after buttering him up with statements of really needing his expertise, and how good for the company he is, etc.

So how does this dichotomy of honorable and dishonorable forgery companies exist? How does one category not simply trump the other right out of business? It would seem to be common sense, and I am asked this frequently when describing the paradox. It comes down to money and timing, two very typical retail concerns. Numerous academic forgery businesses earn their keep by claiming to be the cheapest way of getting your work done. They can't all be the cheapest, but that is a known obstacle in any field. If the advertising is enticing enough, that is all that is needed to pull in customers. What is interesting is that none of these sites show their prices right on the home page. Many don't reveal what the cost is until the order is placed. Perception always beats reality. If the student sees a compelling banner for cheap papers, he is likely to go with it. Cheaper is better in almost all sectors of retail to many customers. That is why store brands continue to be found on shelves in large-scale outlets. Despite carrying all of the major brands, there is always room for the in-house, and it's not just to hold shelf space. It is because it sells. It's cheap. It's not because it's better. Sure, some claim to be "comparable" to the national brand, but superior? Not so much. That is how it is in academic forgery. These companies don't claim better quality. They claim cheap! Save money and still graduate. Get through college the cheapest way and still have free time. That's the key. As a result, these businesses stay in business.

Timing is key, too. Again, to return to the retail market, think about the big box store on the corner. It is part of the culture of commercialism today that many people opine that they wish they didn't have to shop at the large stores, either because they seem impersonal or because they threaten to swallow up the global economy beginning with the mom-and-pop stores. These behemoths stay around, though, and even proliferate. Why? Timing. They offer all their goods all the time. Twenty-four hours a day and seven days a week. Even on a lot of holidays when smaller stores take the day off for their employees. Just like students forgetting about, and needing, their paper in the next few hours or else, townsfolk forget something on their shopping list, or are up late and are hungry, or maybe they're having a holiday party and need something at the last moment but all of the local shops are closed. Off they go to the biggie down the street. They may say they're not happy about it, but they feel forced to shop there, anyway. Same thing with buying an essay. With online courses posting midnight deadlines, cheaters know they can get that rush paper nearly in the middle of the night. Sometimes, in fact, it is the middle of the night if a paper is due at 8:00 in the morning. Who is open right then? Who can get the job done immediately?

Rush outlets! They are the second part of "Cheap and Easy!" Rush papers available is a mantra to many paper mills. For a little bit extra, they can get that paper to the student within an hour or two. Better yet, peruse our collection of quality papers right now and pick the one that suits you. Pay, download, and print, and you're on your way, they trumpet. Can you blame the student? He has less than two hours left before the make-or-break paper he needs. He hasn't started it, or has a serious case of writer's block that is growing worse by the minute. Enter the dishonorable competitor. They stay in business not because they're good, but because they're cheap and easy.

Hence, competitors and honorable forgery will remain a hot topic in academic forgery for the foreseeable future.

7

Is One Sitting on Your Desk Right Now?

The Forger at Work: *I have a fun little two day stretch in front of me. Three orders arrived in my inbox nearly simultaneously and they're all for the same topic. According to the instructions given I can tell they're also for the same session at the same school. Fun. Since I don't have a tight deadline, I mean virtually anything can be written in a couple of days, I think I'll take my time and have a little experiment.*

Not only am I going to cover this group with the exact same thesis for each paper, but I'm going to use the same source material and passages. The only dissimilar element is that I'll use a different writing voice and style. Like I said, I've got plenty of time to enjoy this. Let's see. What do I know about Christopher Marlowe's version of Faust? *I'll pick something nice and easy so as not to arouse suspicion. The themes of greed and pride will do for some basic coverage. I'm sure they'll get around to talking about these motifs if they haven't already. Paper one will get greed and pride. Paper two will get avarice and hubris (hope he's prepared for that). Paper three will pull it off using love for money and love for self. It's all the same, you see. Just different ways of putting it. Because they are all the same essay, really, I'll just skim through the text and isolate the readily-abundant examples of the kind doctor's interactions with the devil which will demonstrate these two facets of the rather mad scientist. There. Now I'll let the first paper quote fairly good-sized chunks of proof text, the second will get small bits of quotes supported by sharp analysis, and the third just gets paraphrasing. All, though, use the same passages and proper citations. On and on the three ring circus plays out over two nice, calm days and nights. I just pick up when I feel inspired to do so.*

By the time that I get the orders submitted to the clients, which I still do nearly fourteen hours before the deadlines, there are distinctly similar essays in front of me, but each with their own tweak. I know that the same instructor will be getting all of them sometime within the next 24 hours, and eagerly await the results and comments from my customers. Will they get caught? All three students are turning in the same paper. I didn't even bother to change the template for formatting, title page, bibliography, etc. If they do not get caught, will they fare well when it comes to grades? In my opinion, there is no chance whatsoever these are discovered as having been ordered and directly submitted. There is no way. A professor would never be able to tell. This doesn't slight the instructor, whom I clearly do not know, never have met, and never will meet. I am certain he is well-qualified in his field and can tell when an essay is proper and appropriate in all of its technical ways. He will know if the cited passages are approved for using to prove these theses. And he'll see right away if the formatting is correct. But will he know these are forgeries penned by none other than Ossi Chesterton?

No way.

I am right. Within three days I have feedback from the customers. They are all happy. Each paper earned an A. In fact, one of them received an A+. Very nice, and the review from that client put a fairly good amount of bonus money in my account. Even better, the two clients who weren't previously regulars in my fold have pledged to come to me for their future writing needs.

I find myself wishing for the opportunity to try this on a larger scale. Could I put ten papers together and have them all hit the same desk at the same time and still come up with good marks and no doubts from the instructors? How about fifteen? My only challenge would be trying to meet the deadline for that many. At the undergraduate literature level, the papers themselves aren't the problem. I think that professors and adjunct lecturers become lulled to sleep by these simple works. They've seen so many assignments turned in that all cover the basics that they only notice things that are incredibly good or incredibly bad. The rest of the students' works, which cover the high points with virtually the same passages in support and only vary in their writing skills and language, get an easy A or B grade and then it's on to the next topic in the syllabus.

I'll be ready for the next batch of papers that will come along. Hopefully, students A, B, and C will refer friends to me. Four papers are better than three. More money, more challenge, more fun. And as long as I don't throw the name Ossi on the title page, I'll never be caught.

Seminar: "Can't the professors just tell when they get fake papers?" That is a common refrain from typical parents I have spoken with regarding cheating in their children's schools. These are highly-qualified instructors who have by and large received terminal degrees in their fields. They have seen, literally, hundreds if not thousands of papers. So shouldn't they know better? Right away, there are two clear problems with the reasoning behind these assumptions.

First and foremost, the issue of professors receiving thousands of "these" papers works greatly against them. The sheer number of basic interpretations of classical works of literature is more difficult for the teachers than it is for any of the students. This is not the faculty's fault. There are only so many correct ways to write about these pieces, and due to the need to learn the high points in a short amount of time, it is quite rational to deduce that most papers use the same proof texts, lines, and verses. "A rose by any other name…." "My love is like a red, red rose." Surely these have to make it into their respective essays at some point. And there are only so many things that can be said about them. So a proper paper, turned in for a grade, will have these same lines with the same citations, describing why they are important to the theme, motif, etc. Unless they are somehow way off the mark, these typical assignments will be perused and passed. That is the truth. If the professor reads the first paragraph of the essay and it reads just like all of the others he has ever seen, then it's just a matter of looking for the supporting paragraphs with solid topical sentences and citations. With those found, the student takes in an average grade and all is well. So do you still think that the professor should just know?

The second issue with the preceding thought is the whole concept of competitors and honorable forgery covered in the last seminar. Cheaters have their choices of outlets to go to when picking out their assignments. It doesn't take long to realize which businesses are worth doing business with. Sure, the cheap and easy way may sound good once, but only the quality forgers are worth the money. When these paper mills are doing the processing, the results are the standard ones that are never memorable, only averagely successful. As pointed out by Ossi, they will never get caught. There is just no satisfactory way of discovering when an original paper by a student is actually an original paper by a forger, if the essay in question is not spectacularly good or spectacularly bad. As proposed, the entire class could probably turn in nearly duplicate efforts from companies like FraudPapers and the instructor may indeed simply pass every one with an average grade. Lots of happy students, lots of happy forgers, and there appears to be no great harm to anyone.

Here is an analogy that I often use when describing these phenomena. Each and every day without fail, the sun sets in the west. Generally speaking, the sunset is not something that people will run outside to see, or pull their cars over to take a look. That is because most sunsets are very, very similar. They are over quickly and present a pretty, though not breathtaking glimpse of natural beauty. These are the basic assignments turned in by college students. They cover mundane topics that are studied as the classics each and every year. Almost all of the essays written are standard affairs—the everyday sunset. Professors don't even notice these anymore. They read them, see them for what they are, average, and grade before going on to the next one.

Every once in a while, a sunset is spectacular. Crimsons, golds, oranges, all of the "wow" hues lend fire to the horizon. Everyone notices and many people stop. They take these occurrences in deeply, enjoying them. They may even grab others to see the beautiful display, as well. At the end of the day it is a noteworthy event. These are analogous to the great essays that professors occasionally receive. Rather than choosing the same old proof texts, or the same interpretations of the material, some students take the hard way around. Obscure points are plucked out and woven into some greater meaning. These require completely different sources to be used. As with the "wow" sunsets, these are the "wow" essays, and the "wow" pupils that instructors just wait and hope for. Once a student shows this promise and level of accomplishment, he will receive much of the attention from the teacher for the duration of the semester, or beyond.

Now imagine if the sun set in the east instead of the west, one day. Aside from any celestial problems this may cause, or any catastrophic end-times predictions this may incite, the point is that it would be much more than just weird. It would be flat out wrong. Clearly, it would be even more noteworthy than the glorious sunset of the preceding paragraph. Anyone that knows anything about basic daily events would be able to pick out this mishap. It would be a real standout. As you can expect, this is the fairly small batch of assignments that get turned in, particularly during freshman composition classes, at colleges across the United States. They are so off the mark either because of abhorrent writing or just horribly incorrect expositions that the instructor sees it within the first few lines. As with the amazingly good papers, the professor will spend more time reading these ones, too. They will take their time with the red pen and note all of the reasons why the paper fails. Essays of this nature will stay in their minds for a while, too, and may be looked at again when the students turns in his next assignment. If there is improvement, then the subsequent grade will be a bit better. Consequently, the "wow" papers and the "whoa" papers garner the most attention.

When it comes to essays, therefore, the overwhelming majority are not really noticed at all. The only ones taken note of are the great and the gruesome.

So now for the million dollar question to instructors across the gamut of secondary and post-secondary education: is one sitting on your desk right now? And if one is, how can you tell? Though this will be covered in more detail in a later seminar, here are some basics about this challenge.

First of all, is one sitting on your desk? What are the chances? The chances are great. In fact, or to use a favorite forger's phrase, moreover, it is actually likely that every instructor of introductory composition, rhetoric, English, whatever it is called at different institutions, will receive at least one fraud every term. That's right, and is worthy of repeating. Every professor sees a forgery every term if he covers general education requirement writing. It is quite difficult to see this in any other light. Understandably there is a great sense of outrage that results from this claim.

Many professors do not deny the possibility that academic forgery is an active profession. Again, it gets down to common sense. There are just too many mills in operation. Someone must be getting these papers. I haven't once yet met a college level instructor who expressed doubt about the existence of this problem. The thought, however, of themselves actually receiving a forged paper and not detecting it causes varying degrees of consternation and near rage among some. Just because papers are purchased and submitted every day does not mean that they themselves ever got one and didn't know! This is a bit ludicrous. This perception among professors exists because of not only a good deal of hubris, but of the belief that plagiarism and forgery are the same. Once the instructor is enlightened regarding the difference, and how forgers exploit that difference, there is usually some sort of epiphany. Usually. A fairly large group still firmly believes that they would never fall for this sort of thing. The fact remains, they most probably have already fallen for it, and are going to in the future.

To return to some earlier stated statistics, consider for the case study the company, FraudPapers. The typical forger that operates as a full-time writer with FraudPapers creates and submits fifty papers a month. With the number of these forgers, that means approximately 6,000 papers per month, and therefore over 18,000 per college term for the two main semesters, fall and winter—18,000 per term from one company. That number only takes into consideration the full-time writers. From my communications with my account manager during my time in the business, it was very clear to me that there were numerous writers who only took a paper a week, or so. So for the purpose of the discussion, we will stick with 18,000 works.[1] When the search engine results for essay writing companies are examined for actual outlets from which one can order, there are literally hundreds around the globe. Because experience shows that some of these companies may be the same as others, with different names, let us take 100 as the number of paper mills in operation, providing papers across the United States.

Here is the stark math: 18,000 papers × 100 companies = 1,800,000 academic forgeries are submitted each semester at American colleges. Nearly two million essays. When Ossi Chesterton wrote his papers in 2010, 4,599 two- and four-year colleges were granting degrees.[2] Dividing the total number of forgeries by the number of institutions gives an estimate of approximately 391 of those fakes hitting each school during the fall or winter term. Again, each term is three months long, so every month, schools take in 130 papers. Every day? Over four. The larger schools receive the lion's share of those, while smaller schools do not receive as many. So, the professors who smugly claim they never got fooled by one? That becomes difficult to believe, in light of the evidence.

Section I: Studies in Forgery

For that to be true, it would be easier to swallow if the instructor showed actual forged papers that he caught before the student got credit for it. With the amount of circumstantial evidence demonstrating that nearly every teacher of introductory classes gets a paper or two, there would have to be hard evidence in the form of an actual academic forgery that a professor or teaching assistant rejected for them to boldly assert, "Not me. I've never been taken in."

The question of whether or not there is a forgery sitting on your desk is settled. If you teach ENG 101 (metaphor for all of these courses) then there is one in your current batch of essays. Now the challenge begins. Which one is it?

This will take some time. When operating under the assumption that the essays are all valid and written by students in your class, which should be the situation, then things like citations become mundane and easily overlooked. As long as your perusal finds quotes around source material, and appropriate citations given the style requested, and there is a bibliography or works cited page at the end, then all is well. However, there is something that the typical instructor occasionally forgets to double check: is the student using the research sources that were assigned? That sounds like a dumb question. However, it is a great place to start if you are really looking to stop the flow of purchased credits at your institution. All professors come to grips with easily-recognized passages from the works they assign for reading. This is a process of general education. Because the courses are not graduate level, the students are expected to rely upon the very well-known elements in the literature. As a result, the quoted material in students' essays ring true with the educated reader, and he doesn't have to challenge or second guess the veracity of the phrase. He will look, however, to ensure that there are quotations around the words, if not paraphrased, and the proper citation such as page number, and a corresponding entry on the final page of the assignment, as well. This is easy when the piece being analyzed is a drama like a stage play. Each line comes very specifically in Act, scene, verse or line number form. There is no way to cheat on that. Either it is right or it is wrong, and quite usually, the professor who loves his Shakespeare or other dramatist knows these lines by heart. If a line is attributed to the wrong act or scene, it will veritably scream off the paper as being wrong—or faked. That's easy. However, there is a much more difficult challenge out there. It doesn't involve plays, but it still is quite dramatic.

No matter what the publication date of a play is, and despite any changes in pagination made by different publishers, the arrangement of acts, scenes, and lines remains firm. They haven't changed. With general literature, though, all bets are off. Book pages numbers are completely held to the whim or whimsy of the book publishing company. If they want smaller type font, then a quotation will be found a few pages earlier than in other versions. Likewise if they decide to have larger pages with the same sized text. Some books are intentionally printed with smaller pages but larger text. That would push a certain quotation to a later page. If some versions have illustrations and some do not, that will change the pagination as well. One can only imagine how many different arrangements there are, especially for a very popular, commonly assigned piece of classical literature. This is where the question of source material becomes key to detecting the forged paper on your desk.

There are two ways to uncover this: the easy way and the hard way. The hard way is the primary method used in education, and particularly in the secondary education level where class sizes are smaller. This consists of the teacher grading papers with his own copy of the assigned book on his desk. Every time that he comes to a citation in a student's paper, he quickly locates it in his book and verifies it. This actually isn't all that hard if the teacher has either lots of time on his hands, or a smaller class. Most likely, nearly all of the quoted material will come from the same sections of the book anyway, given the fact that he has been harping on these exact important passages during his lectures, anyway. Yet this does take a large amount of valuable time, especially if the papers are especially research heavy. Then there's the easy way.

Providing that the instructor assigned a specific version of the book as course material, every student should be working out of the same exact material. The teacher will order the books to be carried by the bookstore, and that is that. The syllabus will show which books are needed, and usually will indicate the bibliographical information on the list. If this is so, and if the instructor has made distinct mention of the fact that students must obtain this version for their work, then he is at an advantage. Before actually reading any of the essays on his reading and grading day, he can just proceed directly to the bibliography/works cited page and check it out. Are there any essays that show a different version was used? If so, shouldn't it make you wonder why? That is a very clear indicator that someone else—someone outside of this class and this class's bookstore environment—wrote the paper in question. At the very least, it is enough to warrant some suspicion. Why not call the student in for a quick chat? Start things off with a little question like, "Did the bookstore run out of course material?" I would bet that if the student is a cheater, he won't be prepared for that specific question. It most likely never occurred to him that his forger used a different version of the book, at all. It was all properly laid out, with citations and end material. Just as a professor doesn't always think to check this little matter, the typical cheater never would either.

This is, in fact, the single most difficult of challenges for academic forgers. They don't own entire academic libraries of their own. They no longer have access to university bookstores or research libraries. Even if they did, they certainly are not interested in spending any money to get these specific versions that are being asked for. Imagine getting paid sixty dollars for a paper, but having had to spend forty-five on the latest edition of a title. There's no sense in doing so. The forger has two avenues available to solve this dilemma.

The easiest way out is to spend a little time, not money. Due to the internet, many books are available to read free of charge. First, the writer will identify the specific book's information. He will take this to a search engine and look for it. To begin with, he will narrow the search filter to include the words "complete text." If that comes up with a positive hit, then he is good to go. It's just like he (and the student in question that he is serving) has the book right in front of him. He can freely cite any part of the book to prove his thesis. If a complete version of the book is not available, he will simply look again, and eliminate the words "complete text" in the filter and replace them with "preview." This almost always does the trick. Most online booksellers have arrangements with publishers to offer some portions of the book online. This is where the quality forger really earns his keep. In this situation, he knows that only parts of the book are available to read, and therefore to cite from. He simply has to make sure that he posits a theory that is provable with the limited text that he has in front of him. If the assignment, for example, is to describe a character's intentions or emotions, and the preview is limited to the first 35 pages, then the forger pulls a character from the first part of the book, and has no concerns about any others. Similarly, if the paper calls for examples of metaphors and other symbolic language, and most students pick the typical ones found in the middle of a book, the student's forger has to find those elements in the first 35 pages instead. No big deal. This ensures that the right version has been utilized, and that proper passages have been appropriately relied upon and cited. No one will be any the wiser.

The second opportunity open to forgers when it comes to having the research they need is to either depend upon their own books they possess from their collegiate days, or to find "close enough" versions online. In these situations, cracks begin to develop in the forgers' armor. Holes can be poked through their work. As with honorable and less-than-honorable forgery companies, there are honorable and less-than-honorable forgers, as well. Some will go the extra mile and do their best to ensure the academic safety of their clients. For example, if a customer asks for the third edition of a book to be used, and the only one available to the forger online is the second edition, he may accurately quote from the second edition and then go a bit further. He may take note of the fact that the third edition is a certain number of pages longer than the previous, and so add a page or two to citations to assume the made up length differential. Crafty—and somewhat successful. He may even find the new table of contents showing chapter titles and page numbers online despite not being able to read the book itself. From there he can make an even closer stab at the actual page numbers for the citations. Not many forgers will go that far, but it can be done, and is on occasion. As with the first way of dealing with research, these papers will have the correct bibliography at the end. Unless the page numbers themselves are looked at by the professor with his own copy, the discrepancy will not be discovered.

However, as noted, this is not always done by forgers. Those that just use the versions they already possess, or that find a close version online, can cause no end of trouble for those who order from them. They take the assignment instructions and complete the paper using a different version than what was asked for, and that's that. Technically speaking, all is well. The requirements for an accurate and well-written paper are taken care of, and it looks just fine. The customer usually doesn't even notice that there is an issue. The deadlines prevent that in almost every circumstance. When customers order papers, they have to indicate on the order what the deadline for the paper is. Nearly always, first-time customers put the deadline that they have on their syllabus, or pretty close. When the paper arrives in their inbox, there is no time to give it a thorough once-over. There is, though, plenty of stress when it comes to getting it in on time. Usually, and always when it comes to online classes, it is simply a matter of receive e-mail, download attachment, save it to the desktop and then submit it directly to the course portal. Then it is entirely in the professor's hands. It becomes one of the many that will cross that instructor's desk over the course of the year.

It is not a matter of if, it is a matter of when.

8

I Guess We're All
Shakespeareans

The Forger at Work: *I enjoy being among the best of the best when it comes to academic forgery. It makes me feel good. If I can't be the expert in Renaissance Drama in front of a classroom, I can be the real authority behind the scenes of the classroom. Because of my studied expertise and experience in this field, the students don't need to even pay attention during their time on campus. There is no final exam for most of these courses, there are just papers. Why not have the expert write those papers for you? I guarantee good results.*

This is easy for me. Despite the fact that I do not have the pedigree of say, a major Californian university that seems to spawn the academicians who specialize in Elizabethan dramatic works, I definitely have the level of knowledge that will pass muster—and pass muster very, very well— in any undergraduate class on the subject. How do I know? Because I already did this in college, myself. If I received A plus grades, how can I not do the same for you?

I'm thinking this as I delve into the orders queue today. I'm looking for easy papers at the moment. At the same time, I want to do the easy papers that make me feel accomplished. I want to feel needed. So I turn to that bard of bards, William of Stratford on Avon. But I'm having difficulty getting any of those orders. It's not that there aren't a plethora of the assignments dealing with this specific topic. I see them pop up and then go away. Then more pop up and go away. I can't even keep up with the flashing orders on the database. There's the problem. We're all Shakespeareans, I guess.

I shouldn't be surprised. I'm not the only one with the big writer's head. I'm not the only one who thinks he is an expert when it comes to the iambic pentameter. We're one big happy family trying to get scraps off the table. It is a daily fight to get these orders. While I'm waiting, I check my inbox for today's personalized offerings. Wow—high end stuff. Architectural influences on Paris, France's city center. The likelihood and challenges of passing down family-run businesses. Customer service and outcomes in emergency room settings. Nothing I want to tackle this morning. This is, however, what is representative of what gets directed to me specifically. Difficult orders? Send them to Ossi. Off-the-beaten path topics? Ossi will get it done and done well before you can blink. But that's not what is generally available to the average writers of the paper mills. I want something fun, something easy. I want Shakespeare.

    I click on the order queue again. There. Quick! Click on that one! Finally, I've got one. It's like fishing. I sit and sit and watch the waters of the database stream by. When I read that one special name I throw in my line. No bite. So I watch a little longer. Again, the one that got away. Status doesn't help when it comes to the dailies that arrive in the general folder. It's timing. The funny thing is, that is what authorship is all about, isn't it? A writer who wants to be an author may have a great idea, a great book concept, but if the timing for it is all wrong, he won't get published. He remains a writer, not an author. Bummer. Academic forgery echoes this. Anyway, I got one. The fish for my mantle. Its name is Macbeth. Metaphoric imagery? Give me a break—I could do this in my sleep. Any college student should be able to. Wringing the bloody hands? The army of trees? It's almost Aesop's fables meets Broadway. It's gotten to the point where I can almost write the citations without looking. I'm an expert, right? Right.

    When it comes to Hamlet, Romeo and Juliet, Macbeth, *nearly anything produced in the Avon neighborhood in the sixteenth century, I can spit it out to you within the hour. Easy money. And I still get to feel good about myself.*

Seminar: Academic forgery would not exist without the concept, the totality, of the writer's ego. Sadly, the same inner drive that makes authors successful does the same for forgers, as well. There is a subtle yet important difference between being a no one and being a nobody. A no one may work in the field in his which he is trained. He may be the professor down the hall, lecturing tomorrow's finest minds. Yet he toils in anonymity. But he does get the satisfaction at the end of the day (and during the day as he reviews his library and studies research) that he is using his education. He is part of the historical flow of academic knowledge. The forger isn't a no one like that. He is a nobody. He toils in anonymity, all right, because he can't share with anyone what he does during all those hours in his local coffee shop or bar. Worse, he knows exactly where he is. He isn't part of the historical flow. He is simply looking at the river from the bank. This is what really bothers academic forgers. It is knowing that what they are doing is neither a contribution to academia, nor what experts in their field do. Need proof about this shame? Imagine asking an academic forger—and I can imagine this myself very clearly since I lived it for some time—what he's working on, typing furiously in the local café. The question posed is usually either, "Working on school?" or "Are you writing a book?" Because of the yes or no answer expected, this gives the forger the perfect out to just nod. I never once looked up and said, "Oh, yeah, you know what? I'm just writing stuff for kids who have paid me." Not once. I would try not to get into any long conversations about anything on the screen, at all. To make up for the public side of the business reputation, forgers have to stay very inner-focused. At least there is a built in mechanism to support the esteem of these writers. It's the fact that they get to be pretend scholars. Enter the Shakespeareans.

Here is a caveat to all professors, instructors, and teaching assistants of this specific niche of literature. The numbers of forgeries being submitted to these courses, those dealing with the classics whether drama or other literature, is startling. Though the statistics are hard to get at, the experience of forgers shows that these are the most requested of assignments. On any given day, they outnumber all other orders by a ratio approaching seven to three. There is a decided paradox going on here. The requests for these papers is tremendous in number. As a result, forgers see them all the time and have topics and theses in mind for them even before they begin writing. So they are easy. They are so common that a lot of writers break a rule held at most companies and simply send the exact same paper every once in a while. In other words, they are so commonplace that it's worth holding on to several exemplars in an electronic folder somewhere. At the same time, however, because the Elizabethan son-of-a-glover turned playwright has such status even now, forgers feel like they are true experts when they approach the bard's work. So at the same time these orders are so simple, they are equally esteem building.

Forgers are all Shakespeareans at heart.

This should be troubling for introductory level English professors, meaning those that are either lecturers, adjunct faculty, or non-tenured professors. They cannot help but teach these classics in the current arrangement of university studies. Really. Their hands are tied by tradition. Furthermore, it is just as common that the same faculty member will be tagged with having to teach at least two separate sections of the basic class, if not even more. Every college I have looked at and contacted during my research into academic forgery, not to mention my four years on a major campus where I earned my degree, has revealed at least one basic course in Shakespeare, specifically, that English majors had to complete. These weren't optional classes. They were mandatory. Whether or not the student wants to continue to other aspects of dramatic literature such as Ben Jonson or Molière, or modern to post-modern literature, they can't avoid an initial go at William Shakespeare. This isn't troubling for most English majors, of course, because they fancy themselves writers to begin with. But what about the other students? There are all of the undergrads who decide that Introduction to Shakespeare sounds better than a lot of the other choices when it comes to liberal arts general education requirements. At the very least, most college freshman have been exposed to William Shakespeare at some time during their high school years. So it isn't as scary a title, at least, as say Philosophy or Psychology. Those two carry with them the fear of the unknown. Better the devil you know. So a group of friends going to sign up for their first semester band together and pick the same classes, and arrive for their Monday morning section of Introduction to Shakespeare, carrying their coffee drinks and some silly, nervous grins. Probably most of them have their books, although a few brave ones think they know this stuff from high school well enough to not worry about it. The syllabus is handed out, and now the gaggle starts to worry. There are assignments, real written assignments, due in two to four days. They realize, during the very first lecture, that college-level Shakespeare may not be for them after all, and that it may be inaccessible to their skills, knowledge, and determination. They're going to need some help here, even help outside of their circle. This happens over and over and over in colleges across the country.

Somehow, during twelve to thirteen weeks of class work, many of these students find out about paper mills and sign up. They need help, and they need it right away. Forgers are all too happy to comply quickly. After all, they are Shakespeareans. In addition, many fancy themselves experts in other fields.

If there were a limited number of seats available in a lecture about academic forgery, I would recommend that two groups attend. Clearly, any instructor of freshman composition and introductory drama should be in the audience. By this seminar, that should be quite obvious. They should be joined by similar levels of their peers who are history professors. This is an easy call, too. The orders queue has nearly as many freshman level history assignments as it does any others, after English. This is because students, for some reason, have a difficult time grasping the dates and connections that history studies require. As this is being revealed, it is a sure thing that the professors of these courses are scoffing. They are right. This is not a difficult concept to grasp. Much of the freshman level sections only deal with timelines, nothing else. How can this be something that ends up in the hands of academic forgers? For the same reasons described in the example of the group of freshman who chose Shakespeare together. History sounds easy. It is covered in school from middle school on up, if not from even earlier. Despite the fact that studies seem to indicate that American students don't know their history well, compared to students overseas, it is still a comfortable class because it seems so accessible given a freshman's experience. Once the syllabus is handed out, though, the dream is over. The first week shows chapter upon chapter of reading and at least one paper due. Also, from the instructions sheets attached to customer's orders, there is fantastic amount of boring and tedious work to be done in addition to synthesizing all of the data provided. Where Shakespeare appears to be daunting in its language, history is scary to undergraduates because of its dry subject material and sheer scope of coverage. Both circumstances entice students to hop onto the search engine in need of help. And, as pointed out, both genres make the typical forger feel pretty good about himself.

When it comes to the implications of this for college instructors, there is a sad and frustrating conclusion to be reached. The very largest class loads, given to the lowest-paid instructors, are the exact ones that are on the "most likely to receive forged papers" list. This is certainly not to say that there aren't many assignments paid for by upper-level students, and even graduate-level students, as well. It is simply a matter of prevalence. The professors at the greatest disadvantage are the ones at the greatest risk. Instructors at community colleges and small universities often have only a few dozen students. This gives the instructors ample time, if they take it, to thoroughly read and investigate all of their papers. Larger universities, particularly the state-funded ones, may have over a hundred students packed in per section. It is not as if these instructors, and their teaching assistants if they have any, do not read all of the submissions they receive in every section, every week. I am not that cynical and don't believe that to be true, and would accept the ire of any professor who fought against that notion. But are they looking for forgeries? Can they seriously take the time to even think about discovering these? And can anyone truly blame them when they don't?

The academic forgers who consider themselves well-versed in the writings of well-taught dramatists and other authors know that this flaw, this fundamental problem, exists. They count on it. Existing methods of looking for forgeries can't detect original scholarly works of fraud, and more detailed investigations take much too much time for the overworked college faculty. They are the fishers who hover at the dock of the companies' orders river. It doesn't take them long to find their next order, if they set their hook quickly enough. With every successful assignment and paycheck comes the satisfaction of nostalgic academic success. That is an interesting paradigm when it comes to the academic forgers.

Nearly all forgers are college graduates. They have already seen, in great detail, all of the work that they list as available subjects for their business. This is a good thing for their clients. Once upon a time, these fraudulent writers were above average to gifted level students. Customers can trust them because of this. Never mind the fact that paper mills are known to exaggerate when it comes to their writers' educations and honors. That doesn't change the simple fact that forgers know what they're doing. They earned accolades when they were students that they could share with their family and friends. Getting the next "A" or the next scholarship or grant meant a lot to them. The ultimate prize of not only a college degree but maybe a graduation ceremonial walk with a few honor cords capped it all. There is no more bragging or sharing, however, now that they have turned into academia's bane. When the fifth reunion of their graduating class rolls around, they can't eagerly tell peers what they are up to nowadays. But in their own mind, they still seek status. They want to be the expert even if they can't share that fact, and want to be the one everyone in today's classes turns to and actually listens to as they speak. The forgery business is the way in which these former stars return to the campuses in their minds. Most of them still pack their laptops into bags and head onto college grounds and their surroundings to do their writing. It is not unknown for some forgers to officially audit a class as a "visiting student" or to just unofficially drop into different classrooms from time to time, if they're large enough. Next time you get the chance to go into an auditorium-sized undergraduate lecture late in the semester, look for a singleton sitting near the back. Could be a forger living the dream. That's the paradox. They are stars and outcasts all at once. Since no professor is giving them their high grades anymore, and since they want to be known as the accomplished student of Shakespeare, they choose to have other professors rate their work via forgery clients. It's not even enough to get the paycheck when it really comes down to it. The review system that many paper mills offer not only gives the customer the chance to submit favorable comments to the company that result in bonus money, but even more they are encouraged to let the writer know how the paper was received by the unfortunate professor who got duped by it. There is nothing better to an academic forger than hearing the words, or more properly, reading the words, "The paper got an A+!" This is so much better than the person who ordered the paper merely saying he loved it. So what, thinks the forger, if the client loved it? He wouldn't know a good paper if it bit him, let alone understand and appreciate a quality scholarly effort. But when the writer finds out that the instructor gave it a high rating, well, that's the stuff of forgers' egos.

Therefore, faculty teaching introductory literature classes, beware. You are going to see the largest percentage of forgeries.

After the Shakespeareans are done being patted on the back by themselves, their clients, and the unwitting instructors, there is a near dead-heat of three class subjects that vie for forgers' favorites. As mentioned, history papers are found in large quantities. Along with those come philosophy and psychology papers. This is because these three subjects, along with English, make up the bulk of the freshman experience. General education requirements ensure that there are many sections of these available each semester, including the short spring and summer terms. Schools have to provide a lot of flexibility with scheduling to accommodate the thousands of freshmen looking to knock these out during their first year. It is becoming much more common now to find these in the online environment, too. This only helps the forgers by limiting the interaction between professors and their students. Instructors have no real sound method to become aware of particular students' writing abilities. It would be difficult to point at a really sound paper and think, "I wonder if this student is good enough to have produced this work?" if you had never met the student or talked with him other than through a blog. Who knows? Maybe it isn't even the student himself that is posting on the discussion board. There have been stranger things done in the world of academic forgery. The bottom line is that the so-called "gen eds" are where the non–Shakespeareans make their money. If the former group considers themselves the cream of the crop when it comes to writing and literature, this equally egotistical group just thinks of themselves as the professionals. They are simply a different facet of the same forgery jewel.

It still comes down to forgers wanting to be special, to find a way to work in their field. Yes, they perceive this as working in their field. When they can't contribute in any other meaningful, active way and earn their living as historian, philosopher, psychologist, well they can still be the expert. They wedge their way into the para-academic gap between faculty and student. It is a way of staying passionate about their special interests. Many of these forgery faculty members still have their old textbooks and lecture notes, or maybe they continue to purchase the newest editions as they come out. Some actually belong to societies and other groups to maintain their own credibility. They do everything but work in the field in an aboveboard sense. So they forge. The thought of receiving superior grades in college each and every week makes them feel that they are contemporary sources that can be consulted and relied upon. The funny thing is that they still crave the kudos from professors, the same professors that they openly disdain for "getting them into" the forging business in the first place.

What does this have to say about the impact academic forgery has upon the business of undergraduate schools? Not as much as it says about the forgers themselves. The writers believe, firmly and honestly believe, that they are on the same level as the faculty they are fooling, and well above the levels of the students they serve. They need to do that in order to take orders every day. When writer #76197 accepts an order from the queue that asks for a robust interpretation of the dark imagery in Edgar Allan Poe's *The Fall of the House of Usher*, he swells up with pride and laughs to himself. He will show the system by demonstrating his excellent grasp of the material. He doesn't even have to read the material for this one. He lives Poe. He loves Poe. In two hours, he has a "robust" work done, reads it one final time over a martini, and chuckles to himself. He hits the submit button, grabs his payment, and awaits any forthcoming review. Even when it doesn't arrive, he knows he's exceeded expectations. More than anything, he doesn't dare take any time thinking that there were over a hundred "experts in the field of Poe" doing the same thing during those few hours. So this describes what the process does for the forgers. But clearly there is something amiss here. There is a disconnect between what is going on in the forgers' heads, and what is occurring at the colleges that received, graded, and favorably returned the papers. The fact that all these forgers are Shakespeareans, or Poe Perfectionists, or whatever, simply can't be true.

If it were true, then forgers would be caught frequently and students would suffer. If the overwhelming majority of fake papers were brilliant works of scholarship created by experts in the field, there would be a lot of head scratching amongst instructors at the undergraduate level. Every professor wants high-caliber students who will look at things differently from the rest of his peers, and the teacher eagerly looks for one every course. Sometimes he finds one, most times he doesn't. The standouts are just that, standouts. They aren't common. But if there were papers representative of this level of achievement submitted with regularity, now that would really encourage some second guessing. Despite what forgers may think, college professors are not naive, and certainly not dumb. They will definitely suspect something is up long before he thinks that he has been blessed with a gifted and talented group in his 8:00 a.m. ENG 101 class. If large numbers of brilliant papers popped up, there would be more attention given to academic forgery, and with more attention would come fewer opportunities for forgers. So it isn't the case.

Section I: Studies in Forgery

The reality is that the community known as academic forgers are not the experts they consider themselves to be. They may call themselves Shakespeareans. Some may laud themselves as the Lords of Gothic Literature. Or maybe the Heroes of History. It's simply not true. It can't be true. Ph.D. holders recognize Ph.D. level work. If they see it regularly in their freshman-level course, they are going to approach the students who submit the work. They will want to meet them, to encourage and guide them, and to mentor them. Educators love to have up-and-coming students like these. It is a way of celebrating the field in which they work, and in which they immerse themselves. Within minutes of meeting the alleged author of the fine piece of academic writing before him, the game will be over. This hardly ever happens. Only a few professors I've talked to have indicated that they have seen papers that are so high above the level of the student writer in question that they did, in fact, question him. By the time the superior student paper has been submitted, the professor has already identified the student as promising. That is just how college goes. So the general lack of discovery shows that expert forgers are not expert academicians. This really shouldn't surprise anyone. Each and every academic forger thinks they're quite special. They consider themselves special, and gifted. That is an absolute prerequisite for doing the job. There is no way that a forger takes an order with a three hour deadline and produces a passable paper if he doubts his skills and expertise. But does that mean he is truly an expert? Hardly.

In the end, college professors across the United States should still fear and look for the academic forgers' work. This is not because of the expertise that they fraudulently slip into assignment folders. It is because of the opposite. These Shakespeareans, History Heroes and others are producing nearly countless slightly above average essays every day. Whatever the forger may convince himself of, his papers won't be detected because they won't stand out in any truly memorable way. They are found in the slush pile of easy-to-grade and pass efforts. But don't cry, you experts of educational farces.

If it were any other way, you'd be a former student and a former forger. A no one and a nobody.

9

Dissertation Disorder:
I Can't Get There From Here!

The Forger at Work: *It's tomorrow already. I worked pretty late last night. I got involved in taking probably an order or two too much. I ended up catching a few hours of sleep, hitting all of the deadlines somehow. It got uncomfortably stressful, though. The last assignment I did was quite long and involved Adolf Hitler's decision making regarding opening up two fronts during World War II. My paper turned out better than his decision making. That being said, I barely got it in on time. It was accepted with three minutes left on the all-important clock that runs my life right now. What that means is that I only provided FraudPapers' system less than three minutes to spell check and plagiarize check the paper before giving it the virtual thumbs up. It is always an anxious time waiting for the automaton to clear my work in last-minute situations. A late paper, even by one minute, means a hefty fine unless there are mitigating circumstances such as FraudPapers' server going down or some other technological deviance directly related to the company. All was well last night, though, and I got to sleep quickly, counting sheep wearing cute little saddlebags literally overflowing with assignment requests.*

When I wake up this morning, I look at the closed laptop sitting on the night stand. It seems to be telling me something. Oh, no, that's right, I accepted a dissertation sometime yesterday. During the mania of trying to stay focused on paper after paper, I completely forgot about that peculiarity. I open up my company e-mail and there it is, staring at me uncaringly. The order instructions sheet is lengthy. It's full of attachments, chock full of information. Some are guidance sheets from the faculty. Many of them are handwritten notes which the client penned to himself over long periods of time. A ton of them are copies and copies of research sources with pertinent sections highlighted. Seemingly everything but the dissertation itself, though that word "seemingly" will turn out to be important, I suspect. I really should have thought this over, I ponder, kicking myself as I sift through the material. Not only is it a dissertation, but it will require adding information and research to what is already there in front of me. I have to create the missing parts myself, and then do the actual writing (incorporating the alleged writer's voice culled from existing pieces, of course). The gist of the order is that the customer is conducting a research problem involving family-run businesses in Los Angeles County, California. He has been working on this for a long period of time, and has been stuck with "the world's largest writer's block" according to him. He assures me that "most of the work" is done, and that he just needs a writer to string it all together. He makes it all seem so easy, doesn't he?

I don't live anywhere near the west coast, and have no desire to head out to L.A. I stay busy forging most of the time, but I'm not independently wealthy, you know? I'm not about to sacrifice a ton of money that I've worked so hard to accumulate on a fast-and-furious dissertation endeavor. I have committed to the order, however, and there is a very large penalty for cancelling such a complicated one. The customer, and the company, is now counting on me. Also, the pay for this one work is going to be great, all things considered. I start messaging back and forth with the client. It is true, he has no exacting specifications regarding the dissertation's focus. He thinks that with what he has discovered thus far that he is attempting to prove what the likelihood is of families successfully passing on their business from generation to generation. That is a qualitative question that somehow has to be supported by quantitative data. One of the bigger problems overshadowing this is that he doesn't quite have a handle on how to interpret, and more importantly synthesize, the data to present it properly. That's going to be my job, apparently. I think I can do this without holing up out west. The great thing is that the client has gotten it into his mind that I am actually located in the surrounding environs of his location. He thinks I am nearby, and since there is a strict policy against us ever meeting face-to-face, it doesn't matter where I live, and he will never know.

I start spending significant hours working on this piece. That's necessary, and probably obvious. I immediately message my account manager of my assignment, which she already has seen, and let her know that I won't be accepting other orders for a while. She understands.

9. Dissertation Disorder

First, I print out all of the attachments that the client attached to the instructions sheet, and read them over seemingly never-ending coffee. Wow, there's a lot of stuff here. I break it down into actual writing, handwritten notes, research problem information, and research material itself. There isn't enough personal interview data in here, so I add this need to my growing list of things to do. I will have to e-mail and call involved subjects and list their responses as in-person interviews. I will have to create survey templates for accumulating more data from business owners and family members of successful and unsuccessful companies. Then I will have to synthesize all of this. And then there's that problem about taking the responses of all of these people and trying to make numerical sense of it to provide some semblance of statistics. It seems that somewhere along the line of my career I came across a logarithm in an old mathematics text from the 1920s that would apply to this challenge. All I have to do is remember key words from it and search my electronic documents that I have written in the past. Thank goodness for that particular function provided by software. It pops up within forty-five seconds. My writing accompanies the scan of the original source. That will be perfectly useable, I think.

This is maddening, though, all the same. It's not easy money. If it weren't for the money, in fact.... Really, I am beginning to think about reconsidering my future. Maybe just one last paper. Or two.

Seminar: To this point, the seminars have focused on the easy and paradoxically quite difficult to discover forgers' fodder. Generally speaking, most academic forgers do not take on dissertations such as the one described in the case study. But they do happen, and more than some would suspect. The stakes are clearly high, for both the Ph.D. candidate and the forger himself. For the student, his whole academic and later career could come crashing down resoundingly. Not only would he be banned from that institution, but likely all institutions. His credibility would be absolutely shot. If he had already earned the master's degree in preparation for his application, he could never use it to even teach undergraduate students if the word got out. And the word tends to get out. Academia runs fairly tight circles around itself. If he used it to get himself out of academia and into high levels of professional responsibility, say a CEO or director somewhere, then being found out becomes even more public and disastrous. For some reason, these events, those apart from the world of education, garner the most attention and awe when they occur.

Nevertheless, these forgeries do occur, and they are nearly always successful. It is not this author's intention to "out" anyone's work, although putting a typical Internet search engine to good use would probably uncover a few. The thought has crossed my mind, also, that I would seriously doubt that if I mentioned a few dissertations by name, the Ph.D. holders behind these frauds would come forward and publicly attack the forger, thus lending a spectacular amount of limelight to their fraudulent credentials. I haven't seen that happen before, and I suspect that it won't in the future.

To begin to understand this particular aspect of the world of academic forgery, it would be helpful and enlightening to pretend to be the prospective dissertation client, much as has been done earlier regarding the undergraduates. This will help to understand how the dissertation-level client and order is both similar and different to the undergraduate level one. First of all, this client clearly qualifies for liar status, as found in the examples of the fairly good student who just gets himself in a jam when it comes to one paper. By its very definition, the dissertation is the absolute capstone of academic study, and is only done once. Therefore, the repeat qualification required for loser status doesn't apply. There won't be any coming back to the forger for further work. Legacies generally are found only at the undergraduate level. So, a client who is ordering his dissertation for a paper mill is just like any simple, honest cheat? Really? Yes. It is a one-time-go. Then the customer will go into academic hiding with his pedigree and head out into the world of teaching and research. To return to understanding the process, enter into a search bar the words "buy a Ph.D." The results aren't quite as staggering as the ones encountered during the search for typical paper mills and essay ordering sites, and there are many subjects and angles covered which must be vetted out, but it is still quite easy to find what you need. The funny thing is that, mixed in with the opportunities to buy the dissertation are numerous hits from news sources describing the problem. During my time as academic forger there were more than a few scandals relating to purchased doctoral qualifications, and these circumstances pepper search results. Major media outlets report on universities that have been struck by this plague, and fairly frequently denounce fraudulent degree holders by name. As of late, even CEOs and high level politicians have come forward, admitting their cheating.[1] Students at American schools of quality, historical reputation have been forced to reveal their being duped, not only on the undergraduate level, but yes, also on the doctoral level. Page after page of these mingled results face the buyer in the market for his own doctorate. There are even buyer's guides for those looking to start. Basically, there are two prevalent trends in the marketplace.

The first has absolutely nothing to do with academic forgery, and should be easy to ferret out and extinguish. There are actually businesses that pawn themselves off as academic degree-granting institutions that not only "grant" undergraduate degrees and certificates, but also master's and Ph.D. certifications. There is no work exchanged, and no assignments are ever ordered. Simply, a client orders the degree itself. There is a hefty price tag, of course, but it simplifies the process. There is no forgery to ever face scrutiny or risk rejection. It is only a consumer retail experience. In fact, most of these transaction occur as quickly as it takes for the customer's form of payment to clear. Then the "proof" is sent. In just a matter of days, the newly appointed doctor can display his achievement on the wall, on his virtual presence, and on his *curriculum vitae*. As long as no one bothers to track down the institution itself for accreditation, then there should be no real problem for the fraud. That is a big "if," though, and as pointed out, shouldn't be hard to discover. Yet, it is amazing to see that this is not always done. But because no actual writing occurs, there is no forgery. It is plain and simple deception.

What is much more difficult to comprehend is the academic forger's version. Although it, too, relies upon the normative retail functions, this is an entirely different animal, and is exceptionally difficult to detect if accomplished successfully. That is because it involves real academic institutions of distinction. It involves real dissertations. It involves real writing, writing that passes an interested and highly qualified committee. Can this be done? Is this really done?

The answers are yes, and yes.

Given everything that has been pointed out regarding the typical academic forgery situation, it is important to disregard all of that when taking a detailed look at the dissertation level of forgery. These are not the "fairway," safe papers that are being produced. They are not written by the everyday forger. The circumstances are quite different altogether. First of all, the safe paper route is not what is appropriate for the forgers or their clients. That simply wouldn't work. Safe papers are designed to melt into a slush pile of similar essays on simple subjects. Due to their nature, they are hardly ever read thoroughly, being instead scanned and assigned the average grade for their average and all-too-common treatment of the subject matter. This is manifestly different from trying to submit a doctoral dissertation. It is going to be severely scrutinized. It is not competing with a hundred other papers all dealing with the same approach to a subject. In fact, the subject itself is highly specialized, to boot. Everything about it says, "Here I am. Take a good, hard look at me." Even if a customer takes a very long time reviewing and absorbing the material provided to him, there would be no explaining and defending a simplistic dissertation. The faculty would see through this immediately. They would know that the work just didn't qualify for the status sought. That is because they are, or should be, active experts in the field. Questions would arise immediately. "Why didn't you relate this data?" "What were your thoughts about how this lends itself to the body of research extant?" There just wouldn't be enough supporting material, thoughts, or findings for the customer to rely upon and bring forth. He only has what is on the desk in front of him, and nothing else is circling his mind. On the spot, the hopeful candidate would be shot down, and his dissertation would be returned as a failure. His only argument he would be left with would be to beg off the lack of details and request more time. With any luck at all, the committee would actually let him rework it and resubmit it. But they do not have to, and often do not provide this option. So there is no true safe approach.

The next thing to analyze is the forger himself, not just the product. The level of forger must be appropriate to the task. This is not the time for the artful dodger to take hold of your future and provide whatever it is he finds on other people's sites. In other words, you get what you pay for, and the forgery companies involved will do their best to assign their very best to the job. When they advertise that any level of paper can be bought, they do so only because they have certain writers within their organization who have already proven their skills and abilities. They have been with the company for a fairly long time and have great results of which to brag. So companies like FraudPapers know they can do what they claim without any worries. These businesses take a large percentage of the profits behind every order. If they can manage to pull in Ph.D. candidate customers, there is big money to be gained. Unless, that is, the writer absolutely blows the assignment, either by not meeting the deadline, or by providing an inferior product. Either situation would be horrible for the company, and not acceptable to the account managers, their writers, or the hierarchy above them. Because the clients involved are liars (honest cheats), they do not have contacts within the company. They do not have a specific business that they turn to in need. When it comes to initial contact, then, they are just as much at risk as any first-year Shakespeare students who need a paper by midnight and hit the Internet in search of a paper mill that just appears to be a good choice. Their only hope comes from the fact that businesses such as Fraud-Papers make sure to cover themselves. They hold on to their very best writers in the fold to attack these assignments. The rest? They cannot, and will not, ever even see one of these orders. They are not up for bid. For sure, they will never hit the orders queue. Only the account managers even know when assignments of master's level and above come in, typically, and they hand pick the staff writer they think will be best suited to it. Within a day or so, the manager has already gotten the tentative go-ahead from his writer. Then he begins to negotiate in advance with the customer, making sure that details are in line with what the company can provide, and of course what the total costs of the order will be. Only at that point will he send the order to the writer. At that point, the writer still may, and often does, refuse to work on it. Some writers even at the highest staff positions do not like to get bogged down in the long-term projects such as these. It takes up most of their free time and limits their personal life. Some of the best writers specialize in other things, such as only taking new clients' orders, or last-minute high value orders. Most writers actually turn down the doctoral requests. There is no harm and no foul at that point—although the account manager/writer relationship may be on the rocks for a bit. If all parties are in agreement, then a suitable deadline is worked out, which generally runs from three to six months at the very most, and then everything proceeds much like the normal operations forgers know. The only difference is in the communication between client and writer.

Section I: Studies in Forgery

They speak much more often than what is found in the daily business of academic forgery. Never do they actually exchange personal information as this is still banned even in these long-term assignments. However, there is usually at least a weekly electronic get-together through company supplied and monitored e-mail. There is just too much going on for the two to not communicate well and often. As one might expect, too, the Ph.D. candidate gets quite nervous for at least two reasons. First, he already failed to complete the dissertation himself, being stuck trying to write it for a very long time. How does he know that someone else will be able to do so? Second, of course, is the fact that he is leaving his entire reputation open to vast exposure. His security risk is tremendous. There is also the matter of the customer trying to still control the situation, as if he is actually doing the work. Perhaps this helps him to sleep better at night, or feel more comfortable presenting the material when it comes down to it. What it comes down to, though, is the fact that a doctoral degree is not an overseer's degree, it is a participant's degree. He will never be able to hold his head high among his peers, if he can be truly considered a peer.

A question that comes up frequently when discussing this topic of academic forgery is, "Doesn't the student have to meet regularly with his mentor, sponsor, etc.? Don't they have these meetings to show what has been accomplished and what is planned?" Of course! That is, in fact, just why the forger and the client communicate electronically so much. Unlike the typical relationship in which an order is placed, paid for and received, and anything extra is also dictated clearly at the time of the order placement, the dissertation order is much different. It is expected that in addition to the overall writing of the final product, that the forger will regularly provide samples, research findings, data synthesis and analysis, and whatever else the client requests. Basically, the writer is at the beck-and-call of the customer. That is simply how it is, and the top-rated writers understand this. They may complain and bicker in their hearts, and maybe a bit to their account manager, but it is part and parcel of this level of operation. The money offered initially is intended to cover all expenses and reports. These details do not need to be spelled out in advance. When things come up, and they always do, the customer only needs to send his writer a message, and whatever is necessary just gets done. This is why not only the most highly qualified writers, but also the most highly patient writers get these assignments.

Another question typically lobbed at this subject is the qualification factor itself. How on earth do the academic forgers successfully complete dissertations that are of high enough quality and depth so as to be accepted for the candidate to be granted his doctoral degree? The forgers themselves don't have the credentials necessary to do this, do they?

Remember a few seminars about just why forgers get into the business, among other reasons? One of the main factors is that many of the most qualified English majors who graduate from esteemed universities and colleges cannot afford to go to graduate school. They do not have the resources necessary to advance. Taking out monumental loans is not an option for a vast number of these graduates, and the number of grants and scholarship awards for graduate school pale in comparison to those available to these gifted individuals during their baccalaureate days. If they could have, and especially because they truly believed in the myth of the English major, they would have gone to graduate school if they could have afforded it. It is not that they weren't qualified, or hard working. Again, many academic forgers, if not most, are highly qualified, very skilled writers. Work at the master's degree and doctoral level is something that they were prepared to do personally. Doing it for someone else really isn't all that different.

Another advantage afforded these forgers is that the nominal Ph.D. order comes with most, if not all, of the research already done and assimilated. For whatever reason, many doctoral candidates simply run out of energy or belief when it comes to doing the writing necessary to complete their mission. They have huge electronic files of years of work ready to assemble into a cohesive whole, but they haven't done it yet, or they have tried and failed. When they do finally approach the academic forger with the order, all of this information, data, research, and statistics goes to the writer via e-mail attachments. This is not to say that the writing is easy. There are the challenges indicated above. The end result must be excellent in its construct, its appearance, its argument, and its addition to the field's current state. Apart from that, though, it really is paint-by-numbers or connect-the-dots writing. Usually, academic forgers have to take very loosely worded orders from college freshman who don't even know what they want or need, and who have done no work whatsoever that they can offer to the writer. The paper has to be created from scratch. Not so with the dissertations. I have yet to see or experience an entire doctoral work being done from scratch. That idea is left to the realm of the outlets that simply "grant the degree" without anyone doing any writing. So the thought that there are doctoral degree holders out there who hired a forger to fully and completely do the work is ludicrous.

When it comes to implications of the use of paper mills to supply dissertations, it is much more shocking when it comes down to it, when you really give it a good thought. Undergraduate papers that are provided and turned in for credit are bad enough. They indicate that academia is not doing its job to properly vet its students and their papers. It shows that much of the classical studies that universities are built around is perhaps outdated and overshadowed by technological accomplishment. Moreover, there is not a tremendous down side to this part of the business. When a mathematics major orders a Shakespeare paper, or two or three, he passes a class that he not only has no interest in, but which has no impact on his future, either. Even if he manages to land the most enviable position in his field at some point, the discovery that he purchased one of these papers would most likely be a laugh at the water cooler. Seriously, a way-off-topic paper bringing down a career at a think tank or laboratory? Probably not. But a dissertation is another matter altogether.

These papers are how the professionals get their positions. More importantly, it is how they get their positions over other very well-qualified individuals. A great fake trumps an excellent lifetime achievement. It throws off the entire field in which it allows entrance to. Ph.D. holders are the experts. They teach the classes. They write the books. They give the talks and support expansion of the academic realm. When they turn out to be frauds, this realm begins to collapse. Trust erodes. Qualifications become meaningless. And it happens every day.

Because of the process involved in ordering a dissertation-level work, which is so dissimilar to the typical forgery asked for by undergraduates, they are just as difficult to discover, and maybe even more so. As discussed, the candidate is at a tremendous advantage when questioned about his submission. If he has done most of, if not all, of the original research, he is well-versed in defending his information. He is quite conversant with his data and their findings. Also, in the course of research and problem solving he has been exposed to much of what is pertinent to him and his field. Surely, he has assimilated most of that, as well. In the end, it must be remembered that this is not some college freshman who just wants more time for pizza. He got to the doctoral level on his own hard work, efforts, talents and skills. He already ranks above much of his class, and always has. It's just that for whatever reason, he can't complete the writing of his dissertation. The great forgers take advantage of all this preparation and the subsequent, implicit trust that the clients place in them. Just as they hand pick lines from plays to support their assertions in easy papers, they know how to sort through, analyze and synthesize what is before them in order to weave their writing skills neatly in a web of deceit. And they're not under the gun nearly as much as they are with the typical client. Usually the long deadlines afford the writer to do his very best work, and they give the potential doctor a good amount of time to become familiar with his work and prepare his submission and defense. The layers upon layers of fraud involved build up a good looking product. Generally speaking, the committees are not expecting forgery to slip into this arena of academics. There is such a competition for these graduate students that to doubt their abilities would be to doubt the very system that they have arrived from and may be behind someday. Clearly it is a system that requires some more thorough investigation. Academic forgery is a bane that undercuts the education institution at the lowest levels, and threatens both academic and professional credibility at the highest levels.

The implications for society's decisions of whom to follow and respect rest upon eliminating academic forgery altogether.

10

Egregious Circumstances

The Forger at Work: *I've learned to just not get involved in some situations. This is a distinct benefit of being one of the top ten writers in the company (a client of mine recently revealed this knowledge in an order … apparently the company promised him that, for an extra charge, they would give his order to a top ten writer). I get to choose what orders I want to take on and which to run from. Even when I am trolling the tide of the orders queue, which I generally only do when I don't have one of my personal clients to work for, I am in no hurry to commit right away when I see an interesting order. Coffee in hand, I skim through instructions and when I see something fishy, I simply click "decline" and continue my search. I never hurt for orders. So when situations like the next two pop up, I can just dismiss them.*

The first is a high-value order supplied to me via my inbox from the company. Directly from my account manager. It has special symbols and icons plastered all over it. Complex order, bonus. Short deadline, bonus. Sent right to me for my special work, bonus. Given the total dollar amount on the order, it is certainly worth taking a look. It doesn't seem that difficult, really, and I am just about ready to click on the "take order" button. Then, for some reason, I feel compelled to take another look. There it is, in the corner: academic level indicates it is a high school assignment. I had almost forgotten by this point in my career that each order form shows the level of writer that needs to be assigned to it, based upon the level of the order/client. Since I am a top-level staff writer, there is no order that I can't take on, and so don't even pay attention to that little indicator anymore. High School? That's just too much. I click on "decline order." Doing a high school student's work makes me feel dirty, like someone who is trying to push youth down a dark road toward a dismal future. I do not like contemplating that part of my career. Denial is easy for any academic forger, I suppose. I think of myself as a swell guy who gets to help people fight the system. Sort of like Che Guevara of the academic underworld. Not the peddler on the playground.

The second order is unusual on its very face. The order form has a vast amount of text typed in as special instructions. Usually, this space is limited to requests that don't fit in the pre-formatted questionnaire. I usually see things like "I would like only six sentences per paragraph" or "Please don't use more than one quote in each page." Well, the requests from this would-be customer definitely don't fit in any info box I've encountered. It seems that the client wants me to be him for an entire semester. There will be two of him going to school. He will be the on-campus version, and I will be the online presence. We'll never be seen together, and we will have different professors. He says that he is just too busy to balance all of the extra classes that he needs to take. Apparently, he has to graduate as soon as possible for family reasons, and so the traditional course load won't get him through fast enough. He offers to send all of the textbooks, course materials, and password information directly to my post office box in exchange for a weekly paycheck. That's right, almost a stipend for forging. I wonder where I would put that on my curriculum vitae. *It would rival any order pay that I have ever had—and he says that he will reimburse me if there are any necessary expenses that come up. Intriguing. Would I receive tax write-offs? Probably shouldn't tempt the IRS, who might frown upon my occupation. There is the added entertainment factor of the forger taking on various identities. But it is just a little too much for me. The academic forger enjoys the get in, get out type of work, not the mundane, eight hours a day job that this order entails. I'll pass for now, and remain Ossi Chesterton this semester.*

Seminar: It would seem from the outsider's perspective that all situations in which academic forgers are involved would qualify for the phrase "egregious circumstances." That may very well be true. Societal standards should demand that it is true. However, to this class of writers, where fraud and deceit are normative values, society's mores don't apply. There are, indeed, circumstances which go well and above the standard interactions of the field.

The use of academic forgeries by high school students is, if not the most shocking, the most disappointing finding of all. When graduate students are caught cheating, the reaction is outrage mixed with disbelief; undergraduates' activities are responded to with "I knew it probably happened." But when the cheaters are from grades eight through twelve? It is hard to describe or quantify the reactions from parents and teachers. It would be nice if all forgers found this to be despicable and passed on the orders. Many do, given the discussions on company comment boards. But altogether too many take the assignments, choosing these simple papers with their easy money.

With so many competitors on the market today, vying for a piece of the forgery puzzle, it is more common than ever to see high school essay writing advertised. A growing majority of the paper mills run these words in their blurb Internet search results, now. Not wanting to discourage any potential client, the companies announce that they can write anything from any level, high school to medical school. While this may not actually be the case, it ensures that the door is not closed to their site right away when skimming in a browser. It may sound absurd, finding high school papers along with professional school work, but there is a reason why this seeming paradox exists: the high schoolers ordering papers are most likely the same students who will someday be attending the top universities, law schools, and medical schools. Really.

Underachieving high school students do not cheat, as a whole. Based upon anecdotal evidence I have gleaned over many a smoothie with a teen in cafes, I have learned that the thought is laughable. Failing students at that level fail. Or they pass in the "just barely" category. Their expectations are met, that way. Without making any sort of value judgment upon them or their parents' standards, this is just the manner of things at the lower academic levels of American high schoolers. The next rung of students, caught between not doing well and not meeting either their or their parents' standards, like getting Cs, for example, may indeed cheat. These are probably the ones upon whom the responsibility for the typical pictures of school cheating is heaped. Looking over another kid's shoulders at his test qualifies. So, too, does the preparation and use of crib notes for quizzes. How about copying parts of other students' papers, or being a little creative in borrowing sources? Yes, all of the above, and probably then some. But this is old-school cheating. It's not good, but it's known about and will not likely cause the demise of the school system any time soon. After these two categories comes the third group which will comprise the egregious circumstance described by the forger in his case study.

To open, I must say that my research into this matter is not of a cynical nature. I did not believe that a tremendous number of high school students, particularly the high achieving ones, sought outside agencies to gain an edge over their peers. This has, in fact, been my finding. While companies may and do advertise their services to this level of student, there is not a huge market for it, and a large number of the placed orders are rejected at the writer level (to the chagrin of the account managers). Apparently there are some standards among the forgers, some sort of honor among thieves, to coin a phrase. There are enough, though, to keep the avenues open. Two very specific orders from those in the twelfth grade, typically, find their way into the hands of academic forgers each year.

The first batch revolve around some form of independent study that high-ranking seniors are working on. Increasingly, these come from charter schools and preparatory academies. Periodically, public high schoolers will send these, too, but the demand on their end is not typical of what is found in the latter two. Because charter and preparatory schools are fixated upon their graduates gaining admission to the best of colleges and universities, the four years of schooling build steadily toward more challenging, and more independent, school work. By the culmination of their studies, students are treated nearly like the college freshmen that they will be. Many have to design their own term project, complete with research and of course a term paper at the end. That is a lot of pressure to place upon seniors, although it does turn out first-year college students who are ready for day one. The competition and high expectations can be too much for some. It is not as if these students cannot do it on their own. They have already proven that they are up to the task, which is why they are in that position to begin with. Completion is not the issue. The issue is getting the highest grade. It is about being able to put the best product possible into the portfolio. There is the slimmest of margins for those looking to get into the highest-ranked schools and the best programs. This may mean calling in help with tying all the facts up into a solid, if not spectacular, paper.

Ironically, academic forgers usually get compensated more per page for these orders. I generally believe that this is a level of non-provable extortion that is going on. The companies know what they are doing, and what they can get away with. They know all about the customers' motivations and limitations. If a standard order from a college freshman goes awry for whatever reason, it doesn't spell the end for that student. He is not likely to get humiliated if he doesn't pass a paper. Usually the paper is not all that important, either. It takes more than one poor submission to actually fail a college general education course. The client won't be happy, but he can always come back later for another one. Businesses like FraudPapers know that. There is only so much they can charge for this type of client, because if their rates aren't competitive the student will just troll around until he finds a cheaper one. And if things don't go spectacularly when the order is submitted to the class, it is only a small order in a huge orders pond for the company.

Things are different for the high school student who gets involved. The company knows that there is a huge burden on the kid's shoulder. This paper may be the make-or-break for him. If he is coming to an academic forgery operation for his capstone paper to ensure top honors, then things are serious. Quite serious. It is like going "all in" in poker. There is no backup plan; they have reached the inn of last resort, typically. They need a great result, and they need it on time. By the time they have registered online with their order instructions, they have most likely run the gamut of Internet operations, looking for the best one. Not any one will do, because not any paper will do. As a result, all of the leverage is in the paper mills' and therefore the forgers' hands. They can charge anything they want if they present their credentials and products right. If the student balks at the price, they are reminded that if they are at this point, then they need the best help they can get, and the best help comes with a price. They are encouraged to just do the assignment on their own. This is a lark. FraudPapers and others absolutely know that their bluff will not be called. They are right. If the student has come to the point where he is ordering his term paper to be at the head of his class, he has run out of options. Waiting and dithering upon whether he wants to pay for the order only shortens the deadline and raises the cost of the paper. Within a few minutes of going back and forth, almost without exception the customer places the order and pays up. It is a racket that is really akin to protection money, at that point. The alternative to sending the ridiculously high amount of money is failing and having to face parental and parochial disappointment. That would not be pretty, and ensures that orders are usually completed.

The second batch of orders that come in from high school seniors do not involve schoolwork at all. They are the papers known as the college admissions essay, the application essay, or the personal statement or essay. More and more, this type of writing is coming to academic forgers to complete. In fact, the majority of assignments given to forgers to complete are just these. Perhaps it is that students don't feel like they are cheating, per se, when they order this type of product. After all, it is not for a school grade. It doesn't involve cheating or paying for research. All-in-all, it could be construed in some heads to be a morally neutral activity.

The process for ordering admissions essays is similar to ordering a resume. The student sends his transcripts to the company. Then, ironically, he has to submit a personal statement that covers, in bullet-point fashion at least, the high points of his schooling/learning experience. After that, it is helpful if he helps the writer to have a basic understanding of what he likes to do outside of the school when it comes to traditional extracurricular activities, clubs, volunteer opportunities, etc. Again, this is ironic, because he has at this point nearly written his own admissions essay. When this is all sent to one of the writers, he takes on the task of creating a cohesive paper from this jumble of information. Somehow, this happens, and the result sounds like a real-life high school senior who is presenting himself for inspection by a major university admissions committee. It is truly an act of fine creative writing on the part of the forger, which is funny because the paper itself is not really a piece of creative writing.

Or is it?

This is why forgers are receiving the orders of this nature. At the level of the personal statement, expectations are higher than they are for advanced placement English classes. Much is riding on this one communication. With the competition all having achieved similar grades and nearly identical scores on placement tests, the one thing that can help a prospective freshman to stand out is his personal statement. How ironic, then, that this most personal creation is sometimes a fraud? That the one thing a committee thinks they really know about an applicant comes from someone that is just as in the dark as they are when it comes down to it? And to think, if the student in question gains admittance to the prestigious school in part because of a purchased paper, he is a step up on his peers not only when it comes to earning admission, but also to a life of distinction. That's what is truly at stake. As a reminder, a student who is asking for assistance with his personal essay is very often, if not nearly always, a very high-ranking student. He is ultimately aiming at not only the best-of-the-best undergraduate school, but likewise the most respected of graduate schools. He knows that he can do very well in these arenas all by himself. By the time of his registering with Fraud-Papers or any other service, he has received superior grades throughout twelve years of education, either public or private. Or he may even be homeschooled, which would be funny due to the one-on-one nature of oversight implicit in this form of education. The bottom line is he doesn't need any academic help, whatsoever. He probably does not really need any assistance with his admission essay, either. There is such a premium placed upon it, though, that it is enough to cause jitters in even these accomplished students. There is another reason, too.

These top scholars have received their accolades by doing well in coursework and in standardized tests. Both of these things have one commonality. They are long-haul efforts. Class grades are received by doing all that is expected and required during the academic term. Everything has to be done very well, and better than others, but there is ample time to learn in a proper order. Accumulating facts and talents over a period of time enables them to get the grades that they desire. Doing well in junior year mathematics greatly relies upon doing well in sophomore level math. Likewise, science, and composition. Standardized tests are this way, as well. When all of the freshman, sophomore, junior and senior information is learned and stored in the brain, then pulling it out come test time is not as challenging as it might be. The one thing that bucks the trend is the admissions essay. It is not something that is studied for, although one could argue that one does prepare for it all during the school years. But it is different. It is uncomfortable. It can get complicated. And it is a one-time-go. This is a nerve-wracking area for many potential college students.

Not so for forgers. This pressure is what keeps them going. Even if it does come from a high schooler.

This is exactly why the other egregious circumstance described in the forger's case study is so repugnant to academic forgers. The idea of having very regular clientele, of possessing a stable of students who need you, is wonderful. However, the thought of someone needing you to actually be the student is not wonderful. It is downright awful.

This situation does not come up all that often. It is truly an outlier when it comes to the realm of academic forgery, and thus is not a very big problem for academia. That is a very good thing, and should be accompanied by a great deal of relief from instructors and those running educational institutions. This is because it is the most difficult of forgeries to detect, and the most completely fraudulent. One of the easiest ways for a professor to detect when a forgery has been turned in to him is to be familiar with the student who claims authorship of the paper. The more interaction there is between faculty and students, the less likely forgeries are to be successful. It is like living between two houses in a small neighborhood. If neighbor A is always outside and you talk with him often over landscaping or reading the newspaper on the porch, you get to know his voice very well. When he calls on the telephone, it is not necessary to see him face-to-face to become convinced that it is, in fact, neighbor A on the phone. On the other hand, if neighbor B never comes out during the day, say working the night shift or being agoraphobic, and there is no situation under which you talk to him, then when the phone rings and the person on the other end only says, "Hello," then you wouldn't have enough information or context to figure out who it is you are talking to. If it is actually neighbor B's son-in-law or even coworker on the telephone, you would never know the difference.

Imagine if professors had to consider this. There are two situations where this could happen. If the student hired a forger to actually be him on campus, then the forger would arrive at the very first lecture with the required texts and a few notebooks. He may even have his laptop with him so that he could work on other forgeries during particularly boring lectures. When and if he decided to participate in class by asking and answering questions and even lending his thoughts to the course, then the professor would come to know him. Unfortunately, he would come to know him as the alleged student and never know he is being duped. Likewise, when the forger turns in papers, the voice is his, which the instructor necessarily assumes is the student's. By the end of the term, the forger has earned his keep and the student has earned his grade. The professor never knew the difference. Again, fortunately, this doesn't happen much at all, due to logistical problems mainly regarding distance, and indifference upon the part of the forgers who do not care for this sort of work.

What is a growing problem, however, is identity forgery in the online environment. There are no distances to travel for the forgers, and no lengthy lectures they have to attend. They can work whenever they have time or interest. In other words, they are just like any other student. When a student hires the forger to "be him" virtually speaking, the professor would never know, just like in the first scenario. The forger gets the passwords, the proper log-in codes, has access to the online discussion boards, and all of the necessary means of turning in course work. Most online courses require their students to post on the discussion board a certain number of times per week to show their online presence, much like attendance is required at traditional classes on campus. They are usually assigned short pieces to contribute weekly, as well, which involve working on several questions that they must answer in mini-essay form. Then there are several full-length papers that are usually asked for. Surrounding this may be quizzes or tests. All of this is done, obviously, without any personal interaction (physically) between faculty and students. The only way that a professor can truly get a feel for what a student's voice really is, comes through reading discussion board responses. That's not much to go on. And unlike the on campus section, the students can't even raise their hand and offer personal responses or suggestions. Quite clearly, no one knows each other in this setup. The instructor himself could be a forger, for all the students know of him. Hopefully, this isn't the case, although given the information covered thus far through these seminars, it is not outside of the realm of possibility.

Once the professor becomes accustomed to the students' voices online through interaction on the discussion board, which they monitor and often add to as the topic unfolds, it is a bit easier to compare the papers submitted by the students to how he usually "speaks" on the shared conversations. Unfortunately, as this seminar indicates, disparities would only be found if there were actual disparities, i.e. if the student who appears weekly or bi-weekly in posts were actually different from the one putting papers in the drop box. If a student has hired someone to be him for the entire semester, however, there will be a natural consistency throughout all of the course's work, and no reason to doubt what is going on. Advantage: forger and client.

One final note about taking the place of a student for an entire class. A niche has developed in the forgers' world. This area does not involve writing at all. In the world of introductory science and mathematics, quiz-only online environments have popped up. These are completely anonymous affairs, requiring merely proper student identification. As described above, there is no difference whether the student logs in, or he has someone log in for him. With no further identification required, an enterprising undergrad who does not like timed tests passes off his identity to someone else for the duration of the period. These are always found in the forgery databases as "critical" orders with not only short deadlines to begin the work, but even shorter deadlines when started, due to the nature of the quiz. Once a test has been opened, a countdown clock begins, and the student or his alter ego has a set amount of time to finish. Perhaps that is what makes this group of ne'er-do-wells seek help. They may know the material well, even, but the thought of having a timer in the background creeping toward completion unnerves them and prevents their being able to concentrate on doing things well, or giving them the mathematical version of writer's block. For whatever the reason, this is a growing area in which forgers are making money.

And it all begins with the online environment, realm of the academic forgers.

11

Turnitin—Not the Failsafe You Think It Is

The Forger at Work: *There is a flashing message marked Urgent in my company e-mail. Normally, this represents a good thing. It is an opportunity that has been hand-picked by my account manager, Tonya, for my personal attention. This could be anything from a client who has come to FraudPapers with an immediate demand or a brand new customer who is trying us out for the first time. We want those to go to the staff writers who can produce something excellent that will encourage the client to come back to us, along with potentially drawing others to create a cheater network. Unfortunately, another reason for urgent messages is when one of our writers has let someone down and the revisions have come back; if the customer is particularly upset or the deadline is looming, these assignments will often get redirected to me to put the finishing touches on before resending for payment. All of this aside, none of these describe the message that is before me when I open it.*

Plagiarism? Really? You've got to be kidding me! That's the claim, though. The e-mail doesn't come from Tonya or any other manager. It comes directly from the Quality Assurance Department. I haven't heard from QAD since I was a junior writer and was just learning policies. But this isn't your everyday, run-of-the-mill policy violation. It's the big one.

I'm offended, naturally, and know that I haven't done anything wrong. It's probably just that darned system that FraudPapers employs. Every paper that gets submitted by a writer goes through an automated review. Basically, all that means is that it gets sent through an Internet search to determine if there is anything that is directly taken from sources. It doesn't distinguish stealing from proper use. All the program does is use its own little formula to find word matches. Each one it finds is considered a hit. After so many

127

hits, a report is generated which alerts QAD to potential plagiarism. QAD doesn't look into it right away, and generates their own summary that alerts the writer that he is on probation until the problem is resolved.

I'm their current problem.

Did I mention I'm mad? No, wait, furious. I am Ossi Chesterton, Ghostwriter to the Stars. I create the sources that people use, not steal or borrow improperly. The paper in question which has brought this shame upon me is an extremely research-heavy essay on the effect of barometric pressure and the storms of the southern Atlantic Ocean. The client specifically said that eight different sources must be used, and that they had better be used in exacting terms. He didn't want too many summaries or paraphrases, and didn't want partial quotes very often, either. That left me with using fairly large chunks of existing research. I wanted a bonus and a very satisfied client to add to my fold, and so followed the directions to a "T." I don't even need to say that I properly cited everything, do I? This one was a bit tricky, too. It utilized ASA style, which I don't normally work with. I had to fire up my reliable college style guide website to ensure accuracy. All that extra work and I get a plagiarism accusation? No way.

I scan the report after taking some good, deep breaths. Sure enough, it shows that I used a lot of source language. There are hits all over the place. And what do I see next to those hits? Proper citations! That stupid computer program. Wait until I zip off a message to my account manager. It won't need citing; it will be original, all right.

Seminar: Many schools have responded to the recent trend and spike in academic forgery by employing proprietary software such as Turnitin. Especially since 2009, universities have relied upon outside companies like this as their first, and sometimes only, line of defense against cheaters in their classroom. Programs such as these are designed to assist instructors in their efforts to discover when works are plagiarized, and therefore safeguard the academic integrity of the classroom.

In brief, this works by searching the Internet for the phrases and key terms found in a student's paper. Each time an exact match is found, the words are highlighted and considered a "hit." By the time a paper has been thoroughly checked through the Web, a report on the numbers of hits (expressed as a ratio of the words on the page) is returned. The more hits, the more likely the paper is to have been plagiarized. It seems like the perfect way to gain advantage over the forgers. Even disregarding the problems of academic forgery infiltrating schools across the country, it is clear how well this could potentially work. When a traditionally lazy or unprepared student is pressured by a writing assignment, it is very simple for them to overload their writing with copied material from required sources. In reality, however, it is not nearly the failsafe instructors believe it to be. Many of the typical campus cheaters will, in fact, be caught, but the forgers rarely even consider this investigative tool as an issue. There are two distinct problems with this current system, the first of which impacts and annoys the good students even more than it does the poor ones. That is because of the fact that accurately and properly cited papers nearly always come back as nearly- to mostly-plagiarized. This results from the limitation that the system doesn't take citations into consideration. There is no tool to detect that. When a quote is used, and a match is discovered in a database somewhere, it is automatically a hit, until proven otherwise by looking at the reference citation, which requires a human. Because these search engine related products have no way of recognizing what is a citation and what is not, it can't return information on that aspect of the paper. This doesn't even approach the question of whether the citation is in the proper style and contains all necessary facts. Therefore, a very heavily researched paper using many quotes will come back as nearly completely plagiarized. Imagine the implications for many scientific papers that rely upon existing statistics, data, and field research. Or, again, consider the basic Shakespeare or other drama class. When an assignment is handed out that requires students to identify key parts of a play that support certain findings and theses, it is common sense that directly quoted lines would be relied upon quite heavily. There is just no way around that. Professors are aware of this, obviously. They all went through the same thing when they were undergrads, well before the advent of any of these later-day products. If the faculty in question, the one teaching introductory English classes, takes the time to submit these papers for vetting and then takes a look at the reports that are generated, his jaw would drop. There would be so much red on the papers, metaphorically speaking, that he wouldn't quite know where to start. It's not that well over eighty percent of his students are cheating. It is just that the vast majority are doing the work that was asked for to begin with. They are doing the source regurgitation that is so much a part of the freshman experience. The standard response to plagiarism is failing the paper or calling the student in for a discussion of the definitions of academic cheating relative to stealing others' ideas. Either way, this is immediately problematic for the teacher. If he only takes the reports at their word, he wouldn't take the time to hunt down all of the citations. When the student complains loudly and vigorously, keeping in mind that they aren't cheating at all, the instructor is then left looking a bit silly. He dismisses the report when the student contests the finding. If this were to be repeated nearly a hundred times per assignment per section, the waste of time and resources would grind the syllabus to a halt. No lecturer would be able to stay on schedule and on task with those problems every week.

The second issue with programs of this nature is that they do absolutely nothing to deter the best forgers. This, also, can be broken down into two reasons.

To begin with, the top academic forgers do not rely heavily upon research and quotations. They create entirely original works, each and every time, with only enough quotes to provide relevance and satisfy expectations. When it comes to academic forgery, time is of the essence. Each forger lives and dies, idiomatically, by the clock. Often, orders are taken at the last minute for deadlines only a few hours away. As discussed, this is because the money for these orders is much better. It is very difficult to meet these timeframes if the writer has to track down research that comes from multiple sources. This is particularly true of assignments that ask for quotes and research from hard copy books. Online copies of the requested books are generally easily available on the Internet, but it does take some time to find them, to make sure they are the right edition, and then hope there is a sample of the text to read. Even if everything up to this point works out, the lack of the entire book can frustrate the forger. He then has to make sure his thesis matches up with whatever material is accessible. It is writing in reverse. Therefore, it is much better and easier for the forger to limit his reliance on external sources. As a result, search engine software won't turn on them when they are done writing and submitting the work. The forger, and the student himself, have very little to be worried about. Writers are more interested in producing a cohesive paper that flows from start to finish, and then plan on inserting quotes wherever they fit best. This limits the use of quoted material, and hence limits the findings of a plagiarism program.

Second, the retail side of the forgery business ensures that the very same detection systems are in place to oversee each company's writers. For FraudPapers, and for most of the quality paper mills, each and every paper submitted by a forger has to go through a quality assurance or review department before it can be sent to a client. This results in a slight delay for the writer, who is fighting the clock already. However, it is usually very slight, as the entire automated process usually only takes one to three minutes to make it to the company, enter the database, be run for plagiarism issues, and be returned to the writer. Either a message accompanies the paper's return announcing a bland statement of "The paper is ready for your client," or there is the dreaded e-mail that comes all by itself. The frustrating thing for forgers is that, like the quality students who properly use and cite their sources, they have done nothing wrong, either. They will most certainly win their appeal back to either their account manager if they are lucky to have that direct contact, or to the quality assurance department if they do not. But the time this process takes is unbearable. Even though the accusations of plagiarism will be resolved, a missed deadline is always punished. The punishment can range from fines that are deducted from the writer's payment, to a reduction in writer status level, to being fired altogether. All because the automated review simply stated that there was a lot of quoted material.

All of this stems from the fact that forgery is a retail business. It is just a series of interactions where a customer steps up to a counter in virtual reality, orders a product, pays for it, and expects it to be what he wanted. When there is a problem with it down the road, the customer complains and wants something done about it. The last thing that a paper mill wants is a dissatisfied customer. If clients are constantly returning papers because an instructor rejected it for cheating by stealing source work, those ordering the frauds come right back to the companies, demanding their money back. Thus, outlets like FraudPapers probably vet their work even more so than the colleges themselves. However, because in the end both universities and forgery outlets use the same precautions and methods, forged papers are in instructors' files right now, gathering dust. They will never be uncovered as forged until the forger speaks, or the client squeals.

Section II: A Few Fine Points

There is a positive side to this form of investigation, which perhaps many instructors haven't considered. Not only does heavily researched material get detected, but also a very low-level version of academic fraud: the pre-written or "canned" essay.

Recalling the lessons of competitors and honorable forgery, this is a growing problem on campuses. An interesting set of circumstances is leading to more and more of these particular forgeries hitting the school market. The intersection of expediency, ease, and price all come together like a bad car deal.

The first part of this is expediency. Student A awakens from last night's party in a stupor. He recalls that he has a paper due that very day. There is a problem with that discovery, though. He hasn't started it yet. He didn't buy all the books for the course that were dictated by the syllabus. He hasn't attended many of the lectures and has very little in the way of notes from the instructor himself. And now he doesn't have any time left. Lucky for him the class accepts online papers in the drop box until five o'clock tonight. That gives him a maximum of four hours to get this thing done. Clearly, that is not enough and he has to look for another way. When he turns to the online paper mills' websites at the dorm's computer, he is looking for the words "Fast Papers!"

Student B has been attending class all along. He is fairly well-rested this morning, having had the ability to wake up hours before his peer. He has known about the paper that is due today for quite some time, and has already written everything but the bibliography page. He is in no hurry and takes the time to go down to the coffee shop before finishing up. By noon, his essay is on its way to the digital drop box, and he is on his way to his next class. There is not a great deal of urgency on his side of things.

Ease is the next part of the equation. Student A is in even more of a hurry now. The clock is ticking. While Student B gets ready to press the submit button, he is stuck looking at search results. It turns out that even the fast papers advertised are going to take several hours from when he begins the registration process. Then he has to make sure that his topic is able to be covered by a writer from the company he chooses, and then there is always the possibility that no writer takes it and he languishes in the orders queue until it's too late for him to get any kind of a grade. He solves this by going to a web site that claims that papers are already available for immediate purchase. All he has to do is peruse the existing papers library, which is broken down by subject and topic, and pick one. This he has time for. It will be easy, after all. He clicks on review papers and types in his needs in the search bar. Within 3.9 seconds he has twenty essays to choose from. They all look great, and have the title page, the text, and a bibliography. All the citations are done and there are good sources noted. All is well as he picks one and sends it to his shopping cart.

Ease for student B, however, is only accomplished by the fact that he has been working steadily all along during the semester. He didn't procrastinate, and because he has attended all of the lectures and took notes which cemented things in his mind, he has a good grasp of the material. Regarding material, he not only has all of the books required, but has kept up on the reading, so when he went to design a thesis he already knew it could be supported by relevant and reliable information. Over a week-and-a-half period, he has put everything together, and took the time to review his style book for proper citations and grammatical issues. All is well with him, too, now and his version of ease is settled.

Now comes the third part of the clash between fraud and integrity: price. Student A was not only lured in by the words "Fast Papers." It wasn't enough to quell his worries when he saw that pre-written papers were available. Given the choice between a few different sites and companies all offering virtually the same things and promising the same results, he had gone with the finding of "FAST, CHEAP PAPERS AVAILABLE NOW." He found it on a great, big, orange sliding banner on a newer-looking website. Student A doesn't have time to read all of the fine print, but he knows that the dollar factor finalizes the deal for him. The web site reminds him of how much cheaper it is to just pick an essay that is already written than it would be to have one of "those other companies" attempt to put something together that you can't see for even more money. There's no haggling, and apparently no catches. Each paper that he clicks on immediately shows him the cost. There is not even sales tax or handling fees. Before fifteen minutes are up, Student A has found his new essay and it fits the bill in every way.

Price isn't even a consideration for Student B. The price he paid was taking the time and making the effort to work diligently. It is the money he spent on coffee when he was studying. It's late-night pizza just off campus when he just can't stare at the computer screen one more time. He has paid his price, all right, and in all of the right ways. None of this even includes the cost of his tuition, which won't even phase him until after classes are done for the year. It is a nice difference for him, as compared to Student A. When he spends money, he gets something for himself, truly for himself, in return. It is the college experience that students who work hard get; it is satisfaction with enjoyment. Every once in a while he will go to the computer and find a text book or something for school and pay for it, having it shipped right to the dorm or apartment, but again, that doesn't represent the price factor that the cheater is having to consider.

Here comes the positive side of things for instructors. Student A turned in his paper to the digital drop box for his class. He thinks that he has gotten one over on his professor, and doesn't even think about the assignment at all after he sends it. Truly. He forgets all about it because it wasn't his to begin with. There is no worry about grades, and he knows it was turned in on time. Breathing a sigh of relief, and maybe congratulating himself on his resourcefulness, he heads to the convenience store for a pre-party snack. After all, there's a major sporting event tonight. He is utterly shocked the next day when he gets the news in his student e-mail account. He has been accused of plagiarism, and his professor wants to see him tomorrow. A quick click brings him to the class page and his grades for the semester. The essay has gotten a zero. He is in big trouble, but can't understand how it happened. The university's reliance on commercial software has done its job. Never did it occur to Student A that if he can find an entire paper online to read and buy, then it is even easier for search engine programs. It doesn't have to shop around or evaluate expedience, ease, or price. It just scans for words. In this case, it found a match. An exact match. Word for word, it is the same paper that was bought the day before. Within seconds, the professor was notified that this cheating, highly organized plagiarism, has occurred. He only has to decide upon the censure that will be delivered to the student in question.

As optimistic as this may sound to instructors, recall the fact that this seminar concerns itself with how these programs are clearly not the failsafe expected. Despite the fact that Student A was caught and identified as a cheater, there is one problem that neither Student B, nor his instructor considered. At the same time that Student A received his notifications regarding student academic conduct violations, Student B did, too. The professor is baffled at the name highlighted on the report he has received. He doesn't have all of the details yet, but the statistics are clear and pointed. A very high percentage, relatively speaking, of Student B's essay has been taken from others' material. In fact, there are enough hits that the spreadsheet indicates the likelihood of plagiarism to be high. This can't be, thinks the instructor. The student is one of his better ones, someone who is always prepared for class and contributes original ideas regularly during lectures. He seems anything but a copier, but the fact is right before the teacher on his monitor. Without too much more thought, however, he sends the same warning e-mail to Student B that he sent to Student A.

If the instructor is shocked, Student B is quite nearly in shock. He had looked forward to checking his grade on the site, expecting no less than a B plus, maybe. The first thing that pops up is his course e-mail account, with its dire warning of an academic indictment for plagiarism and misconduct. He is now on probation, at the very least. Then he goes to the grades page and discovers that he has received a zero. It's for real. He has really gotten accused of cheating and is going to be punished for it. How can this be? There's got to be some mistake, here, he knows, but he just doesn't understand what happened and how it took place.

Back to the instructor. He is thinking the same thing. There's got to be some mistake. After grading the rest of the papers, he can't shake the feeling of disbelief and a growing sense of uncertainty. He pulls Student B's paper from the drop box and takes a look at it. It looks like he would have expected from a solid student. Everything is appropriate. There is a good and interesting introduction, a challenging topical question, and ample proof in the supporting paragraphs. He checks the citations and they look like they are appropriate, and are represented accurately in the bibliography. When he compares the plagiarism detection software's report over this particular essay, he finds what happened very quickly. The hits are all from the quoted material that the student used in his work. However, the paper in front of him shows quotes around those words, and citations directly attached. There are no problems; it's just that the program found the quoted text in its online search. He grades the paper an "A," enters it into the grading system, and sends an e-mail to the student, informing him that the report of plagiarism was a mistake.

The lesson and implication for schools across the United States are stark. When relying upon breakthrough technology like plagiarism detection software, instructors are at a huge disadvantage. This can lure them into a false assumption that cheaters will be caught. Plagiarism can be stamped out and detected easily. Unfortunately, this also applies to good, honest students as well, as demonstrated above. The net catches tuna and dolphins at the same time, so to speak. There is no way that it can't happen. At that point, a number of instructors will make their decisions about accusations and punishment based upon what they are receiving in reports. Not all teachers will have the luxury of knowing their students well enough to second-guess the hits shown. Worse than that for these overworked faculty is that they will have to deal with false positives by listening to, and meeting with students who face suspension for cheating that they didn't do. As if the professors weren't pressed for time already, they are now forced to turn their attention to yet another avenue.

Perhaps worse than all that is the fact that even as search software discovers those who purchased whole papers, and those who are honest, it misses an all-important third group: students who use honorable academic forgers. The original papers completed by forgers run through the checks and balances easily and quickly. Since the same product was used by the forger's company prior to ever sending the essay to the customer, it ensures that the submission won't be detected as being potentially plagiarized. If a student has avoided the used car scenario of buying papers, he will most likely pass right on through his college core classes. This is the conundrum of thinking that universities have a program that is a failsafe against those who would defraud the world of academia.

12

The Internet and the Ease of Forgery

The Forger at Work: *I'm bored. The winter semester is over, and most of the students I deal with have departed their campuses for the year. I'm not surprised. They are not the most serious of pupils, as evidenced by the work I do for them. They're not the kind that hangs in there to do the sprint sessions of spring and summer terms. There are still orders available, but much of what is coming in is found in the general order database, and they are, well, not profound works. I guess I'll comb through them every day or so.*

Finally, here is an interesting one that will keep me busy for a few days. Great! It is just up my alley, or up any forger's alley, because it will involve some detective work in the online world. The sources necessary just can't be found in any bookstore, or easy-to-find databases. It's not your typical piece of literature that will pop up as a "read sample here" book. And no, an e-reader won't help. Fun, fun, fun. What I'm dealing with is a comparison of racial views of British society as discovered through literary examination from the 1700s to the 1900s. The caveat is that I can't use racist material. No rants or personal statements. They must be exemplars of societal judgment through the years.

The Internet is where this stuff is proven. Historical documents? No problem. I don't even need any specialized memberships or log-ins for curator sites. Typical search engines should guide me through a multi-step process of finding the original documents themselves, from which I can quote and cite properly. Going to these lengths, finding the actual works on their own rather than in anthologies will score extra points, and not only for me with the client. The professors are actually hoping that students will do this. The academic forger will actually ensure that the student will shine in the instructor's eyes, and will only grow their reputation. I hope this student can handle that, since he will probably be garnering more attention from his teacher in the coming weeks.

So there it is. Two searches and following some interesting links has led me to scanned-in copies of the first pieces I need. Wow. It talks all about the savages of a certain dark continent. Apparently the author's society, not just the author himself, sees these people as not people at all. They are not even to the hunter-gatherer state. They are the animals. Given the fact that the document does not attempt to convince through persuasion or proof, it is an accepted norm. Exactly what I'm trying to show in the essay I'm getting paid for.

I'm off to a good start.

Just like that, I'm off to the 1800s, seeking objective coverage of the same area and groups of people, but in a more recent context. O.K., now I find out that they may, in fact, be people, but they are naturally a lower class of human altogether. Slightly human, therefore. Naturally not as smart as their counterparts, one of whom is doing the writing, and again not attempting to bolster his presentation because he is presenting this to a world that clearly already believes him. At least the opinions have progressed, somewhat. I have to remember that I'm still dealing with very old manuscripts, unearthed conveniently through my Internet search engine. I can quote with ease, and impress my client and his overseer with my historical discoveries. It's fun to list the dates of publication in the bibliography. It makes me feel like a real scholar, which I need during these boring terms.

Just for fun, I'm taking a few extra hours on the paragraphs covering the 1900s. The Web has simply given me too many easy hits and links to follow. I don't want to use any of the easy sources that everyone else may use. They could grab those from their local library or bookstore, and that's not acceptable to me. First, it's just too hard. Actually go to the library? No way. Not when I have a computer and a pot of coffee. Academic forgers make their easy life look difficult, not their difficult life look easy. It's all about the ease of forgery, and that's where technology comes in. I'm able to dig a bit and come up with fairly rare monographs from lesser-known authors who still represent well their culture of the time. Take that! You're about to look good, student client of mine. Great job ferreting out the real meat of the sociological writing of the day. You're on your way to a wonderful grade, and a real stand-out effort. Don't mean to put too much pressure on

you, but if I do, you can always come right back to me to look just as good
as I've made you. And I really hope you don't catch on to my secret.
  The Internet is my best friend. It makes life easy when it comes to
fraud.

Seminar: As the Internet grows, bastion of research that it is, so
does the ease with which writers can find sources of information. This
is a good thing. It is convenient that, for the first time in history, writers
can conduct research on far away civilizations and historically removed
documents from anywhere there is wireless access. For those who are
trustworthy and do their own work, citing their sources, this is a great
advancement. But this very same technological marvel cuts the other
way and supports the trend in forgery.

Academic forgers become experts at using this tool. The good ones
can take a topic that they have only passing interest in, create a thesis,
research, analyze, synthesize, and produce an order in under four hours.
The length of the paper is not an obstacle, either. There is a lot of writing
that can be done to "connect the research dots." When these papers are
produced for undergraduate level students, this is quite enough for a
very good grade. After all, many writers are displaced academicians who
hold variations of *cum laude* honors from distinguished universities.
They know what professors will find to be quality work, and can reach
that threshold without arousing too much suspicion. Never has academic
forgery been so easy. The next few seminars will briefly deal with various
aspects of this development, much of which information has been covered or can be gleaned from the previous discussions. There are certain
peculiarities, however, that should be highlighted.

Regarding just how using the Internet for research impacts academia, there are three findings. On their face, these would appear to be
varying levels of difficulty, as they yield results that are quite disparate.
They will also result in completely divergent grades for the clients. Unbe-
knownst to the students, there is absolutely no significant difference in
workload for the academic forger, and the thought that the writer could
pass one level off as more expensive as another is indeed a poignant
reminder of how fraudulent the business is in every way.

The first way the Web can be used to ease along a paper from a mill
is one that is employed by the real students every day. Nearly every

search of a term or definition that can be found in a student's syllabus shows a link, and even a partial definition right away, that leads to a very broad understanding of the subject. This source is an absolute no-no when it comes to academic papers. When used and cited (even properly), a student's paper will most always get either rejected by the instructor, or will be marked down so heavily that a passing grade is almost unachievable. Everyone knows what this particular source is. It is an open-sharing site where anyone, from intellectuals to outright liars, can post their research and information about a certain thing. This may educate readers about who signed the Declaration of Independence, or who played on the 1919 Chicago White Sox. It may get as involved as a brief survey, or not even a brief one, of the fourth dimension, or an analysis of the genome project. Oh yes, anything can be found. It is right at the fingertips of someone who would like to learn about a new topic. Exactly because of this ease and seeming scope of coverage, many people believe that this ready information is both accurate, and based upon solid research.

Some are.

Many are not, representing individuals who want to be seen as a specialist. It is much like wanting to see oneself in print. They can proudly point to the web result and say, "See, that's my work." Thus, the cynicism regarding using the findings as a reliable source. Thus, too, the rejection of it in students' papers. Yet it is done every day on campus. The Internet and ease of finding these sources makes it just too tempting, especially when a deadline is looming. Sadly, this same fallback position that gets students in trouble occurs many times when they turn to academic forgers for assistance. Let's face it. By their very nature, the forgers are always looking for a shortcut. They do not want to spend a lot of time on any one paper. The luxury of time is not always on their side, either. So the Internet with its easy "research" results gets used. Often, parts of the text from these sites are directly cut-and-pasted, leading to discovery on the part of the professor, and accusations of plagiarism. On the other hand, occasionally forgers will cite the site as a source, and this ensures outright rejection and the dismissal of at least one of the student's counted sources. In this scenario, the easy way of technology has failed both student and forger. The student fails the class, or at least that assignment, and the forger is usually docked money when this is related to the company's complaint department.

12. The Internet and the Ease of Forgery

Another example of the ease of forgery due to the Internet is the mainstream work of the academic forgers. This is the exact circumstance that makes cheating so easy, and which lines the pockets of forgers everywhere. Even when specific sources are listed in the syllabus as "must-use" research in a paper, this doesn't make it any harder on the writers. Because of the wide-ranging availability of texts in the online environment, there is no added burden to the forger. In fact, not only is there no additional difficulty, but it actually makes it easier for him to do his work. He doesn't have to dig for real, original research. All he has to do is type the title of the book, and perhaps the author, into a search bar. Voilá. Several links to the book pop up. At least one of them will lead to a version of the work that includes previews, or even full text versions. If the latter is true, then anything can be proven as far as a thesis goes. This is especially helpful when the forger is writing the same paper for several students. Yet, even in the case of only previews or partial chapters being shown, that is still enough. The writer will use those bits from which to craft a thesis. This is backwards writing and works just as well. Instead of creating a thesis statement and then combing the book for "proof," the forger simply arranges the bits and pieces, looks for some sort of commonality, and draws the conclusion from them. He easily has his proof and sources. When he is done with the writing, he clicks on "book details" or whatever wording the site offers, and lists all of the bibliographical information necessary for the works cited page. It will appear to both the student and the professor that the genuine sources were consulted and properly utilized because that is exactly what happened. The only thing that is not suspected is that the student didn't do the work. And the funny thing is that the customer thinks that this professional use of research sources was somehow more difficult for the forger to accomplish. He ends up paying more for each source utilized by his writer. He gladly pays up for such quality. What he will never know is that because of the Internet, this wasn't any more difficult than if the less-than-reliable broad-based site was consulted.

The third example of just how easy the Internet has made things for academic cheating is the one described in the forger's case study. Even the most obscure of sources can usually be found just as easily as the above two scenarios. When a particularly difficult assignment comes up from a zealous professor teaching a general education course, or if the paper is actually from a high-level course that requires such work, the Internet is not only the forger's best friend, but is perfectly acceptable, also. When handing out these tasks and asking for students to really examine documents that are contemporary to historical events, they already know that this is not physically possible. Many of these sources only exist in museums or research libraries and are not readily accessible to the students. Therefore, the professor expects the class to participate in "extensive" Web research. He will grade higher for papers that demonstrate reliance upon not only a greater number of sources, but also their accurate insertion into the web of proofs written, if you would pardon the pun. This, again, makes academic forgery so easy and reliable. The experienced forger who has achieved staff writer status already has bookmarked avenues of research and source material that will easily guide him to relevant historical research. It is not as if he has to go to a bookstore's website and hope for the best. He doesn't even have to do a generic search within a tool bar. The writer of note already has handpicked sites that will give him the documents that he needs, and which will astound his customer and impress the instructor. At the same time the client and professor are happy, the forger is even more pleased. He has reaped much more than he has sown, because the allegedly complicated order has been given to him on a premium basis. The client has had to pay much more for this type of work. The catch? He thinks it is difficult because it looks that way to him, and the company has told him so. But this is a well-crafted lie. The Internet has made this type of forgery just as easy as any other.

Is there anything that should tip off the various levels of instructors that encounter these forged papers unknowingly? Not really. It is expected that this type of research is more difficult and time consuming, first of all, but there is a serious Catch–22 to this. During a typical thirteen week long semester, which represents the main terms of Fall and Winter, it is perfectly reasonable for faculty to believe that all sorts of great and novel sources can be found. There is much more time between and during assignments to assume that exhaustive searches can be done to uncover historical material that can undergird academic arguments, bolstering them and supporting the thesis chosen. Obviously, though, if this is not only possible, but likely, for the students, it is even simpler and easier to achieve for the everyday academic forger, not to mention the truly accomplished one. Therefore, the assumptions made by the staff work against them.

By contrast, when the shortened sessions of Spring and Summer terms arrive, with their halved semester lengths, and these sources are relied upon, the professor is still not likely to point the finger. There is a fairly implicit understanding that by and large, these terms are populated by much more serious and astute students. Most of the lower-achieving undergrads have a difficult enough time getting things done during a normal semester, let alone having to do the same amount in a vastly shorter time period. They are not normally found sitting in the desks between May and September, as a rule. That means that professors may rightly assume that the students in their sections can handle the workload well, and still excel. When apparently difficult-to-find materials are noted as sources in a term paper, then, it is not a stretch of the imagination to see this accomplishment as proper, even expected. In reality, he has been duped by his own seemingly valid assumptions.

Either way, the cheaters and their forgers have remained ahead of the staff. They stay on the cutting edge, working against, and even using the paradigms that have been established in academia thus far.

One more way in which all of this benefits the life of the academic forger, and which ensures that the business is not only here to stay, but will continue its growth trend, is that the writers can be anywhere in the world at any time. There are no limitations to where a forger may live, relative to his clients. This is very good news for the student, first of all. He is not limited to local writers. The consideration of where a forgery company is located, even if he were actually able to deduce that fact from the web site, doesn't usually ever come up. The customer can browse essay-writing companies for as long as it takes him to become comfortable that he has rightly chosen for his specific needs. As long as he can access the business, he knows the business can reach him. Everything is done electronically, anyway, including the class itself much of the time. And because of the prohibitive business policies in place at outlets like FraudPapers, the customer could never find out where his writer is located if he wanted. That information is not only unavailable, but completely irrelevant.

The only time this comes up is when the student truly believes that he has reached a local business with nearby writers. Sometimes he will message the forger and ask for a meeting to go over some details, or maybe he wants to deliver a specific version of a book that he wants the writer to use. Again, the forger will refuse. First of all, it is strictly against every paper mills' policies for these types of encounters, to the very best of my knowledge. There are just too many complications, from mad clientele to the remote possibility of academic sting operations. Secondly, the writer very well could be on the other side of the earth from the customer in question. Imagine the surprise on the client's behalf if he were to discover that his essay writer didn't even live in the same hemisphere as him! But with the Internet and easy availability of research sources and submission methods, this very well may be the case.

It is the perfect example that is representative of the Internet and the ease of forgery.

13

Online Classes and
Proof of Ability

The Forger at Work: *I often wonder why colleges are making it so easy for me to do my work. They might as well come up with a direct grant that they can send me every so often. I remember when I attended college, and had to come to campus for my initial testing process. I had to demonstrate my writing ability in an essay to show whether I should be passed along to the second semester of Freshman English, or whether I should be relegated to the first and would have to complete both sections.*

Nowadays, I am getting assignments from students who only have to submit the initial essay along with their other basic information online. Online? Really? How convenient is that? Certainly it's convenient for me, anyway. I have one in front of me right now. This is laughable. The student is all worked up about it. He only has a week to get this done, and he is worried that he won't get into the second section of the course, which would cost him tuition money on an unnecessary class. He did well in high school composition classes and doesn't think he would have any problems showing that, but the pressure of the one-time essay to prove his ability scares him. And yes, he has only a week. "Please remember that, dear Writer," he informs. "This can't be late, so please tell me early if you can't make that deadline."

A week? That means I have six and a half days to start writing.

While I'm waiting on this one, I take another. This comes from a well-prepared, planning type of student. Where the above kid is a liar, I can see that this guy is going to be a loser. He's already getting ready to employ me as "his writer" if all goes well. It turns out he has to. What he wants me to do is prove his ability to a professor. The class is Introduction to Drama, and is the first course in a long line of online sections he plans to take with this very same instructor. It must be a small college. Anyway, he wants to show that he is a good writer who is well-informed and able to produce high quality work. So he wants to get off on the right foot with me in his place. Once I show his teacher just how talented the student is, and let him become familiar with my writing style and voice, I can then do all of the coursework that comes up, semester after semester. Now that's how it is supposed to work. I like these sort of setups. He's my client, and I'm his writer. He needs me to prove he's skilled, and then I have to help him keep up the farce.

In both situations, I'm the voice of the next generation of student writers. I'm their proof of ability.

I've had to help some kids get into college itself before. Well all right I didn't have to help them, but I was in between orders. I sharpened up their backstory and then set them off on their own. But this? I'm setting them off, all right, but not on their own. I'm not part of their backstory, I'm part of their future. I don't care how many papers of theirs professors hoard and compare—like they're really going to do that, anyway—it won't matter. They will all sound alike. No way they're forged, right? No one would go to such lengths, would they? That's the problem, though, isn't it? The student may not realize it when I write that first essay for him, establishing just how well he can pen the prose, but then he has to live up to whatever expectations come along with me setting the bar. Now this is truly the challenge for the student. If he is rude with me in his request instructions, I may do him a disfavor.

What if I really put some serious effort into the paper I send? That first essay will not only get him placed into the second, more advanced section of the general education circuit, but it will get attention, too. What if he turned in a clearly graduate-level paper? How about a cutting-edge angle on his thesis, top-notch analysis in his supporting paragraphs? Well, now, he may be in for a bit of trouble when he gets to class that first time. He'd better be able to back up that reputation he now has.

Otherwise, he may need me to remain his online proof of ability for quite some time to come, and my prices only go up as semesters drift by.

Seminar: Again, this aspect of forgery has to do with the ease that the American culture expects. Therefore, in keeping with today's students' claims that they are too busy to come to campus, online classes have become status quo in many schools. The issue here is that the professor has no idea who their students are. For all they know, each student that is in the class is a truly gifted writer capable of producing unusual brilliance in a short period of time. This is because he has no way of assessing the base writing level of a student. Even if an instructor attempted to get students to produce a writing sample, submitted online, within the first day of class, it is clear that with the magic of instant messaging systems, even those tight deadlines can be met easily, albeit at a higher cost, by FraudPapers.

In the most extreme of situations, as described previously, the professor doesn't even have the guarantee that his students are even who they say they are. All the roster shows is a student name and identification number. Some only show the name, with no other information at all. Presumably, if a student knows the login and access codes, then it must be that student. That would be the default assumption, and why wouldn't it be? However this notion has been dispelled by the stories of more desperate, or conniving, clientele. It is just as likely that the student on the roster not once participates in the class at all, having paid for a stand-in for the entire semester.

While this has begun to change the cheating landscape of American colleges, there is a much more sinister situation that needs to be addressed, and will be the focus of this seminar's direction. The change has a foundation, and that is called high school. That's right, high school.

And how could this be? With much smaller classes and general educational reputation established by students with their teachers, this would appear to be very, very difficult. Forgers may take on some of the assignments that come up, particularly during the latter days of schooling as students begin preparing for college admissions, but generally speaking the cozy environment of high school precludes getting over in this way. However, there is a subtle shift that has gained momentum when it comes to this level of academia. It is the new wave of virtual schools. For whatever reason, public, private, and charter schools seems bent on adopting online academies. Whether these are aimed at one or two classes for students to catch up, in a more traditional way akin to summer school, or they are the new, expansive, form of entire grades being available in the cloud, the trend should be disturbing to both parents and educators. There are varying levels of oversight, and even the most closely monitored situations are too open to cheating to be worth their while. The temptation is too great.

Section II: A Few Fine Points

This is not to say that fraud is rampant. The door is open, though, and outside assistance is too readily available. Even in situations where the school promises one-on-one, or highly personalized guidance or tutors, it is truly a lark. Both scenarios lack the personal interaction necessary to gain vital information about the nuances of the student. His style, knowledge base, and core ability cannot be garnered effectively. Even where the instructors are not only highly qualified, but very experienced, and above all dedicated to their cause, that is not enough. As in college classes where all of the above are present, the odds are stacked against them. Particularly in the case of students who are enrolling in online schooling, even where they are young, say freshmen in high school, there is a glaring fact that is not considered for its depth of implication. If the students are this comfortable and accomplished with negotiating both the cloud and the traditional web, they spend more than enough time online to have come across the paper mills. If they use the service a few times, and get those middle-of-the-road papers that are available, who will be the smarter? Or, more cynically, if he finds out early enough, what if he gets through in this non-traditional environment almost entirely on the coat tails of others?

Or, even more cynically, what if he has such a good experience with the academic forgers that he shares this information and develops cheater networks?

At the very same time that there may be an audible gasp from educators who are reading this, it should be pointed out that many of these instructors are also all too familiar with the hardships and difficulties of teaching at the high school level. Whether public or private, the complaints and frustrations have been boiling over in recent years. Underfunding, overcrowding, lacking in resources or cohesive planning, all of these have become a plague. It is difficult to point accusing fingers at a lack of direct oversight when it comes to guiding students in a one-on-one way. Not only does this provide opportunities for academic fraud, but it also can create students who are just as frustrated as their teachers. Their attitudes can be directed by just how well, or how poorly, they feel they are treated. At the emotional maturity level high schoolers are at, it is easy to react negatively to what is perceived as apathy or hypocrisy. If they perceive that they aren't valuable enough to be directly interacted with, or that they see a school advertising that their online environments are not only cutting-edge but provide personalized programs for their students, and then they are failed in this matter, they just may fight back against the system. It is an early version of the myth of the English major.

Just as college graduates who were fed the liberal arts diet find that life afterward may not be as rosy as they were led to believe may turn against the system by forging, the same may come to pass with younger kids. If they feel maltreated, or not treated, or even duped, they may see cheating as a natural reaction. They would be taking what they consider a justified stand. This could impact their decision making throughout the rest of their academic experience. It could change just how they view authorities and hierarchies. Twenty-somethings with this mindset would not make very good employees, would they? Not to mention the fact that they would enter the workforce expecting easier results, and not knowing how to properly operate within social employment norms. These represent worst-case scenarios, of course, but the implications and possibilities are clear enough to mandate a close look. Does this mean stamping out online coursework altogether at the pre-college level? No, not necessarily. But it is vital that educators and parents become aware of this growing problem. Without acknowledgement of this trend, cheating will grow. There is no better environment than the online one, when it comes to academic fraud. And the forgers are ready to assist.

14

Word Processing, Properties, and Copyrights

The Forger at Work: *I almost committed a cardinal sin a few minutes ago. I was in a rush, having two deadlines coming up pretty quickly in the rearview mirror, not to mention the back of my mind where I subconsciously start prepping these papers, and nearly hit submit a bit early. O.K. slow down, double check.*

The last thing I look at before sending the order in is the Properties tab on my word processing software. It is still showing me as the author. Well, it is showing my alias as the author. Either way, that won't work, and could get me in significant trouble. I have already created an author's account under an alias, so my real name will not show up even if I forget. But still, I need to do two things every time I write.

First, I have to remember to clear the properties field. It should show that there is no author at all. This, too, though, isn't what the final product should indicate. That's why I include in my standard e-mail at the end of the submission process a reminder for the client to go to the properties field and put in his name. Also, if he saves it to his computer or drive, the field should automatically populate with his name. Perfect. Nice and easy, as long as I follow up on these things.

These technical things wear me out. It's not that they're that difficult, but they require actual use of tabs, and arrows, and drop downs. This slows down my groove when it comes to writing. Also, they become routine tasks, which is why they are much more likely for me to forget and overlook while beginning to think about other things.

One thing I do think about occasionally is a seemingly small detail, but which works its way into my mind. I type up papers, which are my original content. Doesn't this automatically give me copyright? It is my intellectual property, right? The moment I slap a title up on the page and begin working, it's mine, mine, mine. I can do with it what I want. So if I send it to someone and don't dispute ownership at all, aren't I relinquishing my ownership? Then, technically, if the client downloads it, and adds anything to it on his end, is should be his work. That makes sense. Then, doesn't he create ownership and therefore copyright to what is now his work, by default? So can he be accused of turning in someone else's work? It's a fine point.

It's probably a fine point I shouldn't think about too much. Distraction is not good for an academic forger.

Seminar: At this point, one thing should be obviously true: academic forgers are professional liars. That is to say, the best ones are. They have the most on the line, are the busiest, and are involved in the more lucrative end of the business. That doesn't mean, of course, that they care about their clients or their wellbeing. It's just that the personas behind forgery are fairly diabolical. They didn't get into the field for above-board reasons, because, well, there are no above-board reasons. It is an under-the-table enterprise, done in hiding and shadows. So why should these writers even concern themselves with these details? It is all about control. Again, it is not for anyone else's benefit. If a customer were to come to the company and state that he is up on a plagiarism charge and faces suspension or expulsion, it is not as if he can present his case to a legal team of FraudPapers, for example. Certainly the forger himself is not going to come to the aid of his maligned client, offering advice on how to beat the system. These things, the little pieces behind the scenes, are just intriguing to the writers themselves.

The concept of word processing, since its inception, has been a double edged sword for students and the faculty that teach them. Once the Internet and this software merged and joined forces, college became a lot easier. Papers could be worked on in stages, saved, and reviewed as time passed. Once sent in, professors could save them, print them, or otherwise review them. The entire process became streamlined. As described in previous seminars, there are numerous loopholes and caveats that need to be considered, as a result.

Sometimes students are accurately determined to have been cheating. This usually only involves calling his bluff. There aren't many other avenues through which to pin someone down. Fortunately for schools, in the majority of instances a few threats of grievance committees and possible punishments is usually enough to get the student to confess; he can then avoid much more than academic probation. As forgery advances, and its use becomes more popular, however, students have a few last-ditch lines of defense, all because the technology behind writing, storing, and submitting papers has become so accepted and little scrutinized.

Smarter clients, and perhaps those who have a stronger and closer long-term relationship with their own writer who lets them know a few secrets, use a few strategies to protect themselves before submitting essays to their instructors. First of all, and maybe the most obvious of methods, is to download their orders directly to the hard drive of their computer. Although that initially does nothing to mask the author, it is the necessary first step in getting this accomplished. If they only pull it out of a drop box, for example, and submit it from that medium, any properties information that was saved on the forger's end gets sent along. At the very worst, that means the writer's real name is on it somewhere. Or maybe his alias. The very best situation is an empty fields domain. But if the student wants to use this in his defense, he needs to put himself in the position of author. By saving it to his hard drive, he can now edit the work. Once that happens, the moment he begins changing anything—even if he simply were to delete a character and then replace it—the computer believes he is the author. The program should automatically fill his name into the file. Artificial provenance has begun.

This may seem a trivial endeavor. Certainly it is, under nearly any circumstance. Where the student is accused of plagiarism, though, unless the professor has uncovered an exact, or quite nearly exact, paper somewhere, it remains an accusation without hard proof. At the very beginning, the student can begin a vociferous "I'm outraged" defense which may ward off future punitive actions. As simple as it sounds, the student can point to his name that was allegedly saved electronically at the time of writing. If it is, he claims, this shows clearly that he wrote it. That would definitely seem definitive, in the absence of any hard proof to the contrary. The student could then go completely mum about the allegations, and in his silence not manage to make himself look nervous about the whole thing, which may give him away.

What about the other features that are automatically created by software that attaches to the file as it is being written? Dates of editing the file can indicate when the paper has been worked on. Wouldn't a very late date, especially one that indicates the final writing as being done only minutes before submission indicate that something may be wrong with the situation? Shouldn't there be history showing the various modifications and "sessions" that went into writing the paper? Not if the student is thinking ahead. All he has to do is turn off this tracking feature. If he claims that, to save space in his files, or even because he accidentally chose these settings, he has the change-tracking features turned off, there is again not much that can be done.

If for some reason, there is an additional author listed in a document, too, there is still recourse. Many students are now opening up the sharing features of their files so that they may be edited by others. It could be that the writer who is supposedly cheating is actually a good student who knows the power of having someone else look over their work and help him with small changes. That would explain any "help" that is showing in the history of the document.

Apart from any of these issues of word processing and its various properties issues, can a student rely upon vague interpretations of copyright law? I have actually heard from my clients that they would "invoke this right" if push came to shove. It seems to be that there could be some legal reliance upon the copyright act of 1976, in which federal law recognized rights of authorial ownership from the moment of creation, rather than having to wait for official copyright or publication.[1] So when a writer puts pen to paper, or fingers to keyboard, whatever they produce is theirs, legally. So even if someone else wrote the paper, if the student who bought it modified it in any way, it is his intellectual property. Unless, that is, the forger would want to fight this in court, claiming his rights under creating the work initially and substantially. I don't see that happening. Is all of this really possible?

I would suppose that, in extreme and unusual situations this could be relied upon. That is not to say that it would be successful, although the challenge would be intriguing. I have not experienced, or even heard anecdotal evidence to substantiate any of these challenges, but would enjoy seeing how it all turned out. If the stakes were truly high enough, it is possible that a student could go down this path. If there were no hard, viable, proof to the contrary regarding his cheating, and if the student were, for example, a graduate student who would stand to lose both his academic and perhaps professional standing, wouldn't he want to fight with everything he had? I would think so, although it seems a ludicrous route to take. One would hope, cynically speaking, that such a high-level student would be more than able to hide his wrongdoing well enough to avoid having to defend himself in the first place. This would start with choosing a more honorable paper mill in the first place. Research-savvy graduate students and Ph.D. candidates would be more than qualified to determine what qualifies as a quality source for academic forgery, dismissing the less-than-professional outlets before committing.

It's time to look at just what the implications are for student and academia regarding these details and processes.

For students, covering their tracks is necessary. It should be just a part of their activities. Perhaps the liar, that is the honest cheat, who only uses a paper mill for one essay one time just to get through on an assignment, could be properly expected that they might not think of this. On the contrary, this client may also be highly-charged and paranoid about the whole situation, and therefore be more prone to checking and double-checking any avenues of being traced. So, there's that. This would likely apply to legacies, as well. They could be excused, to use a figure of speech, for not knowing well enough to clear the properties of their purchased work before turning it (and maybe themselves) in. Or, again, they may be overly worried, if it is possible to be, and scan everything thoroughly, trying to stay a step ahead.

For the losers, and those participating in cheater networks, it would be much more likely that the customers would be well-versed in taking care of themselves. They use the services over and over, and their experience only grows their knowledge and awareness of these things. The longer they cheat, the less likely they are to make mistakes and create problems for themselves. Especially in the well-organized networks of friends who go to the same outlets, there is a great deal of sharing information and tips. It makes their lives much easier, and results in very few complaints to the forgers and the companies that employ them.

What about how this affects the schools themselves? Should they be looking for the minute details and add them to the arsenal of forgery and plagiarism detection? No. It is a nearly fruitless and wasteful endeavor. Attempting to "prove" cheating through these methods is not a good use of time, efforts, or resources. Even where circumstantial evidence is discovered, it is not hard-and-fast proof, and the students, as discussed, could fight the claims and hold out to the bitter end. And they probably would succeed, in the absence of an identical essay being out there to discover. Professors, and especially the ones on the lower-rungs of academics who may have hundreds of students in numerous sections, do not have the time, and probably not the patience, to look at the properties and history of papers. It is hard enough for them even to read all of the papers in a timely manner. They should be looking for the other indicators of cheating as described earlier. Great papers from mediocre students. Papers that are clearly not in the right format for the class. Rare, or difficult to uncover academic sources for basic classes where the books are already assigned and expected to be used. This is where instructors should be spending their time.

The purely technical aspects of forgery detection only create futility for those who have to look into them with any regularity.

Advantage: academic forgers.

15

The Future of Academic Forgery

Seminar: Even as late as 2012, two years after Ossi Chesterton began his career as an academic forger with FraudPapers, plagiarism detection hadn't advanced beyond its earliest efforts. This is somewhat understandable. Plagiarism is an amateur's game, and usually only occurs among poor papers submitted by poor students, perhaps poor papers submitted by poor students purchased from poor paper mills' databases. Generally speaking, professors, and even more certainly high school teachers, can spot this sort of thing easily. Why high school teachers? They are very in touch with the individual students due to small class size and interactive style found at that level of education. The stilted language that accompanies simple cut and pasting shows itself as easily as if it had been highlighted. This facet of cheating, of course, has nothing whatsoever to do with academic forgery. There are very few commonalities between detecting the two. Regarding the former, there is not much of a need to advance the field. The software and intuition of educators usually is enough. As a result, successful grades based upon plagiarism are typically not granted, and the process is fairly easy to solve for, with one exception.

Even that loophole is found in the academic forger's hands. The tried and true methods of discovering this sort of cheating involves proprietary software mentioned earlier in the book. It is really just a search engine, so it can be used by anyone, even if they do not own a copy of the software itself. All that has to be done is to pull up the student's essay, choose the "select all" function of the word processing program, and paste it into a search bar. When the enter button is clicked, any substantial matches will immediately come up, uncovering the fraud. Alternately, if the plagiarism-finding program is used, a detailed report will be generated, showing the numbers of exact hits along with the likelihood of the paper having been borrowed from somewhere. So to reiterate, when it comes to traditional cheating, this is enough. But what about the aforementioned loophole? Forgers who regularly do work for a cheater's network find themselves submitting papers to clients who are at the same schools but in different sections of the classes requiring essays. In this instance, the writer may turn in the exact same paper for these students. If the sections are taught by different instructors, they will be none the wiser. Software can't find this circumstance because it is not made for it. Never do these papers find their way into the online environment where they can be discovered as being identical. The only possible solution to this is a purely hypothetical one. If every single essay turned in to a department were uploaded into a database, then this would allow instructors to compare them. However, there are serious limitations that will likely preclude this. First of all, to ensure an exhaustive comparison, papers could not be searched until every single one were submitted and entered into the database. Otherwise, an outlier could sneak in at the last minute, escape this method and receive a grade. This system is impractical.

To begin with, if there were multiple sections of the same course and each of them assigned the same essay at the same time, then all of the instructors would have to wait until they assured each other independently that all papers were in the database. Secondly, reading and grading the papers would have to wait until that go-ahead was given. Professors would have no way of beginning to grade the works as they came in. That is the preferred way of grading, of course, because it prevents a backlog of essays needing to be reviewed and graded. Delaying the process would cause instructors to continually fall behind more and more as the term progressed. If this did happen, then by the time final papers were turned in at the end of the semester, it is possible that course grades would not be issued for weeks afterward. That simply would not be acceptable. Not to mention the fact that the teachers would already be beginning another semester at that point. It would also eliminate any time for the faculty who are attempting to earn another degree such as finishing doctoral work, or any independent research or writing. The burden in academia is weighty enough, especially at the adjunct and lecturer level, that adding to it in such a manner for such a limited gain would, and should, be shot down.

In addition, a forger may take on the same order literally dozens of times for schools across the country. It is not as if there is a dearth of basic English essays all covering primary literature pieces from bland, general angles. Just like that, he submits the same paper to each and every client. Despite the fact that this practice is generally frowned on by the paper mills, it would be laughable to believe that the writers are all toeing the line. Some of the outlets actually bar the writers from engaging in simultaneous submissions in their policy notices. What is especially interesting is taking a look at how they prevent this. Each and every paper submitted for an order by the forgers gets stored in a database. A simple search and find program found in the company's computer will show these copies in approximately three seconds. Forger found, forger fired. Sound familiar? The businesses involved in fraud have the ability to do what the schools can't. No matter where the order is coming from across the globe, it is entered into a centralized database. It doesn't matter what country or school the essay will ultimately find its way to. Prior to that, it makes its way to the centralized database. And any forger in the company's stable could have grabbed it and completed the work when it was placed. But guess what? There is no special treatment—all of the work submitted for payment gets entered into the centralized database. The word, the idea, that gets repeated over and over is "centralized." One company such as Fraud-Papers continually monitors tens of thousands of papers at all times. Day and night, and in each and every time zone. There is a reason that the forgers' deadlines and submission dates are all displayed in the twenty-four hour clock based upon Greenwich Mean Time. That is how far-reaching this monster is. But the universities can't accomplish this. If a major university on the West Coast receives an essay that is simultaneously turned in to a major university on the East Coast, there is no way to find the match. As described, it wouldn't even matter if the same university received the same essay turned in to another department all the way across campus. Even where colleges have banded together into conferences, there is just no resource that is utilized in this manner. The essays do not exist in the same collections, and are therefore not searchable.

15. The Future of Academic Forgery

Only lazy students with sloppy forgers can be caught through plagiarism software, therefore. The primary method for thwarting them can be accomplished by any individual instructor. When the customer finds a company that sells the pre-written essays they have in their "library" and he buys it and turns it in, he is instantly traceable. Hundreds of hits on a search engine or similar program will probably sway the instructor when it comes to doubting the origins of the paper in question. A stern look in a one-on-one meeting will probably break the student, who in his guilty nervousness would start squawking and revealing their dishonesty. This would occur right before they begged mercy and declared that they would never do it again. And this can be done on a paper-by-paper basis as they come in. Ironically, instructors of online classes have a bit of an advantage in this arena. With around-the-clock submissions allowed, the professor can simply "grab" the paper from the digital drop box he uses, and immediately vet the paper in real time. But before becoming complacent and satisfied with the knowledge of this tool's availability, consider the following.

How does this "solution," the long-relied upon traditional tool, affect the problem of academic forgery in America? The fact is, it does not help the schools who fall prey to this trend at all. They are fighting a losing battle. Here is a good example:

The highly-esteemed Massachusetts Institute of Technology's Comparative Media Studies/Writing site provides their departments a basic understanding and simple approach to attacking cheaters. However, in reality it gives very little in the way of truly pragmatic, rational advice. The key words here are "rational advice." M.I.T. actually suggests that their instructors visit different essay writing services' sites to "[see] what these sites offer … [this] can help us know what to look for and can help us develop strategies for making such plagiarism extremely difficult."[1] Really? This is clearly doublespeak intended to assuage feelings of worry, to say the least, and quite farcical to say the most. All the instructors will find are English papers. They will cover the basics, and they will cover them in basic fashion. There will be no "a ha" moment for anyone who follows the advice given. All they will come away with is a growing certainty and awareness that there are companies who provide papers for sale. Without engaging in the business through placing orders or working in the field for a bit, their knowledge base will not be thorough enough to see realistic solutions. One could excuse the professors for crying, at that point.

Other advice given to those same educators includes entering "unusual phrases or sentences" from students' papers in Google … and well, you know the rest.

The point is, schools across the nation are treating plagiarism and academic forgery as the same thing. That notion absolutely must change. This is a conception that is archaic. Plagiarism is a small problem. It doesn't threaten the overall reputation or reliability of the American education system. Right now, it is not an unfair accusation to state that academia is collectively either in denial of, or even unaware of, the field of academic forgery itself. The thought of some of the American classical education system's finest and most promising graduates turning on the schools and writing fraudulent papers is a sobering one, indeed. If this were an isolated problem, that would be bad enough, and should inspire action. That is what happened with plagiarism. Academicians who cared about the integrity of education saw the problem inherent in deceit, and attempted to stop it. Awareness was spread, and ultimately technology was put into place to aid detection methods. Academic forgery isn't a small problem, though. At some point, nearly every institution will encounter a forger's papers, whether they like it or not, or admit it or not. Further, it is a constantly growing problem. It occupies a niche in the retail market that is finding more customers who are spending more money. It is a tremendous growth industry. If the paper mills were publicly held businesses, they would have to report earnings and trends. Imagine FraudPapers posting consistently growing yearly earnings and profits. Now that would be a laugh. Or a cry. Or at least a wail of anguish. Yet that is exactly what is going on.

The future is not this bleak, though. At least it doesn't have to be. The academic world of the United States simply has to revise their thinking about the problem of academic forgery. To begin with, the issue must be addressed, and addressed by all schools. Large and small, public and private, high schools, community colleges, and universities. Diploma and certificate programs, associate, bachelor's and master's programs, even Ph.D. programs. No one is safe from this bane, and the only effective way of stopping it is to work together openly. Administrators will have to swallow hard and realize that they are not above reproach. From rural high schools to the Ivy League, no one is immune.

In 2012, Richard Pérez-Peña of the *New York Times* reinforced this in his article "Studies Find More Students Cheating, With High Achievers No Exception."[2] He specifically named a prestigious high school, an Ivy League university, and a military academy, all of which had fallen prey to academic cheating. However, there is a serious problem with the conclusion that was drawn. The main observation of the article, and seemingly the position of the educators interviewed, was that students only needed to be educated about what constitutes cheating, because they may not understand that what they are doing is wrong. It allows for the belief that there are some nebulous, or at least vague, areas when it comes to cheating. In other words, ensuring that the incoming freshman read the academic integrity statements will make them stop. How absurd. It still comes down to the fact that the educational world is confused about what the real problem is. It is difficult enough to believe that the students described in the *New York Times* article really didn't understand that sharing parts of papers, i.e., plagiarism, was wrong. But to think that students who actually purchased the entire paper online may not realize their actions violated the university's policies is ludicrous. Yet there is much more of that taking place than there is simple copying. It is just not being identified. And could these schools really say that the clients of academic forgers just didn't know for sure that this is wrong? That it would be solved if only these cheaters would more thoroughly understand the academic standards required of them?

The key? Prevention before it even gets to that point, not mere expectations, or attempts at detection.

As described throughout the book in the seminars, quality academic forgery simply cannot be detected. Where writers like Ossi Chesterton are working, there is no way to find their papers. These forgers are quite possibly the best students that may have once been in your class, educators. The papers are all original, so plagiarism software will not find them. The sources and citations that are used will all match up and be accurate and well-founded. The styles will be appropriate. And in most cases, the resulting essays will be solid, average papers not worth doubting or taking a second look at. They will fly under the radar, while the instructors worry about clearly deficient, or remarkably excellent works. Again, the answer is therefore found in prevention.

This will require the involvement of not only the academic institutions and boards of education, but also governmental oversight. Yes, it needs to go that far. Right now, there is no punishment at all for the forgers. If the student gets caught, he will be subject to probation, suspension, or expulsion by his school. It is possible that this will follow the student into his academic future, especially if he is planning on going to graduate school. Sometimes it will even plague a graduate into his professional future, leading to embarrassing revelations both to the employee and the company that hired him. But even in the case that a cheating student provides the name of the company where he bought the paper, there is nothing that the instructor, or the hierarchy above him, can do.

Most of the larger forgery outlets have begun posting warnings and disclosures right on their home pages to place the blame directly on the students if they submit one of their works. Popular caveats read like this: "Warning: Our essays, including ones already written and those that are ordered from our writers are for use as examples of how to write essays. Students who use these for any purpose other than this understand that they are responsible for any sanctions that may occur. At no point, and under no circumstances are these papers to be submitted for academic credit of any kind."

Some of these outlets may even go farther in their statements. They actually indicate that using their papers for gaining academic credit is illegal and can be punished severely. There is only one small problem with that.

That is because academic forgery is not illegal. Anywhere. There is not a law on the books that precludes the legal operations of paper mills. Even where there appears to be coverage under penal codes, they are too vague to be applied, or only apply to the person who actually uses the essay, i.e., submits it for a grade.

Here is an example, taken directly from the state laws of New York regarding forgery in general.[3] There are several problems. The closest direct tie to academic forgery can be found in definition 1 of Article, or section, 170:

> 1. "Written instrument" means any instrument or article, including computer data or a computer program, containing written or printed

matter or the equivalent thereof, used for the purpose of reciting, embodying, conveying or recording information, or constituting a symbol or evidence of value, right, privilege or identification, which is capable of being used to the advantage or disadvantage of some person.

This would certainly seem to apply. It is easy to declare a forger's work as a written matter that conveys information. It can also be used to the advantage of some person. However, this is simply the definition of the instrument, and does not indicate the actual violation, or use, that would determine criminal activity. It is just a preliminary statement utilized to define words and ideas that will come in the violations section of the law. Those activities that criminal charges could be brought against, are the false "making," "completing," or "altering" of a written instrument. Here's the issue, then. First, here are the definition of those items, again from New York state law:

> 1. "Falsely make." A person "falsely makes" a written instrument when he makes or draws a complete written instrument in its entirety, or an incomplete written instrument, which purports to be an authentic creation of its ostensible maker or drawer, but which is not such either because the ostensible maker or drawer is fictitious or because, if real, he did not authorize the making or drawing thereof.
> 2. "Falsely complete." A person "falsely completes" a written instrument when, by adding, inserting, or changing matter, he transforms an incomplete written instrument into a complete one, without the authority anyone entitled to grant it, so that such complete instrument appears or purports to be in all respects an authentic creation of or fully authorized by its ostensible maker or drawer.
> 3. "Falsely alter." A person "falsely alters" a written instrument when, without the authority of anyone entitled to grant it, he changes a written instrument, whether it be in complete or incomplete form, by means of erasure, obliteration, deletion, insertion of new matter, transposition of matter, or in any other manner, so that such instrument in its thus altered form appears or purports to be in all respects an authentic of or fully authorized by its ostensible maker or drawer.

It's clear from this list what the problems are. For a person to get charged under definition 1, he must either falsely make, complete, or alter a written instrument. The academic forger does not falsely make the instrument because it is his authentic creation that he authorized. He does not falsely complete the instrument again due to the fact that he is the authority behind the instrument. And he does not alter falsely because again he is the authority behind the document. Any and all legal challenges cannot be brought against the academic forger. No matter who orders a paper from him, or asks for him to prepare one for him—even if the forger knows that it will be turned in for a grade by someone else—he has done no wrong legally in the preparation of the written instrument itself. Understanding that a written instrument such as an essay could theoretically be described as conveying value of advancement is not enough. There is nothing specifically written in the statutes that point a finger at the forger which would indicate that legal charges were appropriate.

How about indictments being brought against a student who purchases, and then uses the paper for his gain? That is a little closer to an interpretation of the potential application of existing forgery laws. But is it even remotely possible to bring charges in any case?

Definition 1 would seem to apply, but doesn't. Falsely make? The student who ordered the paper doesn't create the written instrument. So that part is out. The indictment would have to directly prove that he created, in whole or part, a paper and claimed it was authored by someone else. For example, if he were to write a brilliant drama for class and turn it in as allegedly being William Shakespeare's, that would be falsely making. This isn't the situation, though, and the student hasn't even created or altered the document, anyway, so he is safe.

Definition 2 would cover a situation under which a student changes, materially, the document supplied to him by the forger. However, there are still challenges and problems that preclude charges against him. The key issue is that he must do so without the authority of the person who may grant it. If the forger understands that papers he supplies to the student may be added to, or changed in any way, he is granting that authority. That applies to any part of the altering process. Recall that properties of documents are left blank by the academic forger? He expects the student to fill those in. That qualifies as altering. Also, the template cover page that forgers supply does not include the name of the student, the section of the course, or the instructor's name. That all needs to be supplied, or added to the paper. This is falsely completing. But the forger anticipates this, expects that these things will be changed, and has the authority as the author of the creative piece to allow the purchaser to enter this information. So Definition 2 cannot be applied to the wrongdoing.

That leaves Definition 3 under the law: falsely altering. Right away, a perusal of the statute yields the problem. Within the very first sentence, one finds the words, "without the authority of anyone entitled to grant it." The academic forger, because he created the written instrument, possesses the authority to grant the right of altering. It is a retail, commercial, understanding. The customer orders the paper under stated company policies. The main policy is that he will pay for it, and has limited recourse if he doesn't like it. As a result, the forger creates a written instrument that, under policy, satisfies the order's specifications. He then releases the paper to let the student do anything he wants with it, thus creating the transfer of authority. Simple as that, the entire activity escapes any sort of legal oversight.

That, in fact, answers one of the most common questions that I have received over the course of my research. "Isn't that illegal?" And the answer, as demonstrated by the example of New York state law, shows that it is not illegal. It is unethical. It may be declared immoral. Certainly it violates academic misconduct and integrity statements that universities and other schools require their students to sign. There is not much that needs to be proven when it comes to academic misconduct indictments. The sheer fact that a student turns in the work (or written instrument, to use a legal term) of another person qualifies him for the full penalties available. But the forger remains in the clear. He would never even know, let alone care, if the student were caught and expelled. As long as the money was transferred, all is well. And guess what? The payment has to be released to the academic forgery company before the paper is released to the client. So the recourse would be for the customer to complain to the company, who would simply turn around, feign absolute shock and disgust and ask, "What? You turned it in? That was supposed to be merely an example."

So could the client sue the company? Not at all. The contract, implicit as it is, has been satisfied. Paper ordered, paper delivered. I haven't come across even one suit in which the client of an academic forgery company charges the business with wrongdoing. Not once. And this is the way it should be.

The answer comes from a different legality, altogether. The forgers themselves must be shut down. The irony here is that it wouldn't take much to accomplish. First of all, boards of education, and regents of universities, would have to accept and admit the fact that this is occurring even within their hallowed realms.

That could be problematic. These are bastions of education, especially at the highest of academic levels. And yet, they receive papers just as often as any other schools. Once they take this step, though, the process to criminalize the activity can begin. States could begin this effort, although it is shown, and will be demonstrated, that federal law should properly cover this. Because of the fact that in nearly all cases the student ordering the paper and the forgery mill itself are in different states, forged essays are crossing state lines in a virtual manner. Clearly, this falls under federal jurisdiction, then.

Boards of education should bring the findings, and then present them to their congressional representatives. This would start the process. Although federal oversight and governmental involvement is frowned upon by many constituents in the United States, the fact that any bills that come from these investigations only apply to charging academic forgery should be more than enough to convince legislators to act. Imagine the public backlash if congress refused to intervene in the cases of students gaining degrees and access to professional occupations by cheating. It would seem to be akin to be political suicide. That is because it is fairly unfathomable to think that any lawmaker would come to the rescue of an academic forger. It would certainly raise questions.

So, in the end, two things must be understood. First, academic forgery has tremendous implications when it comes to education in the United States. Second, it is a growing problem, fed by basic concepts of retail business.

Now that the conversation is started in earnest, it is time to look for solutions. The first step is to take a good, long look at what is driving writers to become academic forgers. There are still too many graduates from the United States' classical education system that are led to believe that their future lies in academia, only to realize that there are not as many avenues open as they hope. Their disappointing job searches inevitably lead some to explore forgery.

Above all, academic forgery won't stop without legislative action. Until that happens, all we can do is proclaim to the academic forgers:

Stop it.

APPENDIX ONE

Congratulations!
You Made the Book

Over the course of writing for FraudPapers, there were the mundane moments, the mind-numbing papers, and the difficult-to-fathom client requests. Mixed in with those were the downright outrageous, and ever-entertaining orders. Here are three of the more memorable. The first is told through the eyes of the forger, Ossi Chesterton, while numbers two and three are presented in a bit more detached voice.

1. I have forged over three hundred papers thus far in my career, yet I cannot believe what I am looking at on my computer screen. I just can't believe it. It is perfectly understandable that a student would want me to write a paper for him on the subject of romance and tragedy in William Shakespeare's *Romeo and Juliet*. That part is simple and reasonable. I have covered this subject, or very closely related subjects, dozens of times in the past two months alone. What is completely off the charts is the e-mail that just showed up in my FraudPapers inbox.

First of all, the subject line reads, "URGENT CALL ME." Capital letters? Is this customer crazy? Everyone knows by now that capitals letters in electronic communication equate to yelling. No one, and I mean NO ONE, yells at the Ghostwriter. O.K., that part is settled. Second of all, urgent or not, there is a hard and fast rule in the essay writing industry that says there will be no exchange of personal information between writers and their clients. Clearly, this includes the passing along of private telephone numbers. I am not even supposed to let clients know where I am located, either by phone exchange, postal code, or time zone. There are to be no personal entanglements. Therefore, there will be no "Call me." Yet even that is not the part that I can't believe. It is the fact that once I open the e-mail itself and start reading the body text, I realize very quickly that it is not the client who is writing this request. It is the client's mom.

Just how do I proceed with this request, now? It is a very difficult decision. Should I choose good black coffee? Or should I go with the forger's martini? It appeals to my mind that this particular situation may prove to unwind as a tedious, lengthy, problem. I better stick to coffee, then, and head off to make some after turning the computer's speakers up a bit. Although not necessary, I like to hear the chime of incoming FraudPapers e-mails. The sound could indicate nearly anything: client requests, company requests, order updates, personal bonus announcements, and apparently, requests from clients' relatives to call them. I am not disappointed. By the time I am pouring my special blend into a mug, I've heard the chime four times. I'm being pushed by the daily forger's grind, and yet I never rush. Pressure is good, but paranoia is the enemy. I slowly enjoy one sip of java and return to the computer.

Just as I reach for the keyboard, my cell phone rings. You know what I'm thinking, don't you? Is it really that client's mom calling? Now that is paranoia. There is no way that she could have my number. In fact, very few people have this particular phone number, which I use for work. Turning over the phone reveals the caller I.D. It is Tonya Foster, my personal account manager at FraudPapers. Tapping the screen, I intone, "76197 here," giving my writer identification number. I love this part of my job. The prohibition of personal contact is even practiced when talking to Tonya. That being said, there is no way that Tonya Foster is her name. Given the heaviness of the accent, and the curious way she transposes nouns and verbs within phrases, I would bet my next paycheck on her not coming from an Anglo background.

"76197. Were you receiving about order 179934 some e-mail?"

"Yes, I have it in front of me," I respond.

"Do not call that person," she orders. I have always known that FraudPapers snoops through our e-mails, but that was sure quick. "You will be still doing that order, so ensure deadline is met. Is this all clear?"

"Yes, all clear, thank you. No calls, just get the order done. Right."

"Goodbye, then." Click. That was all, and then Tonya was gone. It was almost like she was never here. Working for a prominent essay writing service is like this. It is part spy-thriller, part sci-fi, and always full of drama. When I find myself bogged down in the doldrums of boring orders, a phone call like this one always makes my day. Yes, those phone calls, and this new e-mail. It's time to get back to work. The first thing I do is turn on the latest college top 40 music and punch up the volume. I write best, and fastest, with this in the background. Perhaps it makes my brain feel more connected to the bulk of my clientele. Then again, it also provides me a certain degree of consistency. This is college town bar and grill ambience. The neurons in my nervous system know that when this music kicks in, it's performance time. Off I go, page after page, without hesitating, without faltering. Wait. That sort of makes me sound like a lab rat, or Pavlov's dog. I'll just ignore that for now, but I know for sure that the comparison will come right to mind the next time I write a psychology paper. Another funny moment in the life of an academic forger.

"Dear client," my e-mail response begins. "Thank you for your recent message. I understand that there is a certain urgency to your order, and am open to whatever questions and concerns you do have. However, company policy prohibits our personally communicating by telephone. Could you please send me your requests back to this e-mail address at your convenience? Thank you, Writer 76197." I always try to be as professional as possible when interacting with clients. There are many reasons that this is simply good business practice. It calms down the clients greatly. They anticipate that their papers are being treated by a professional writer. Many even believe, then, that an author or terminal degree holder is doing the work. This, in turn, eliminates many complaints that come up in this line of work. Since the clients are not very talented writers as a whole, as evidenced by the fact that they are hiring others to do their writing for them, they are intimidated by the thought of a degree holder's skills. So they do not question the format, references, citations, or style of the final paper. Those are challenges that I simply have no patience for. I am a more than qualified writer for these pieces of work. If I can lessen the chances of trivial pot-shots at my competence by writing polite, professional, e-mails to clients, it is a no brainer.

Another reason for these communiqués is even more self-serving. As with any other retail business, customers always want the best value for their money. If there is one thing that I have learned in my career with FraudPapers, it is that the clients all seem to know other clients. Just as car buyers post reviews that influence others' purchases, and doctors increase their business through word-of-mouth advertising, academic forgers gain repeat and referral business in this manner. I have had many e-mails from clients that begin with phrases like, "Please be looking for an order specifically for your writer code number that will be about medieval history," or, "A friend of mine told me how great of a paper you did for him, and I would like something just like that…." This makes life very easy, not to mention profitable, for me. I do not have to look in the orders queue for work, as these special requests go right into my inbox for me to select and work from. Then there is the matter of additional bonus compensation for requested orders, and referrals, etc. All of these wonders stem from a carefully worded give-and-take through client e-mail.

Speaking of e-mail, the chime of incoming messages sounds again. Order 179934 is responding. This should be fun. And it is. "Dear Writer 76197, my son is in class right now and so can't give you his information by e-mail. His professor will be mad if he is e-mailing in class. Are you sure that you can't just give me a quick call? Here's my number, again, if you've lost it. By the way, what time zone are you in? Are you near Perth, or Melbourne? Like I said, please get back with me as soon as you can so I can give you new details from my son. He is paying a good deal of money for this paper, and it needs to be just so. Looking forward to hearing from you." So this order is from Australia? And she thinks that I am in Australia, too? That would certainly explain why her boy is in school right now, when it is nighttime on the weekend where I am writing from. How funny. This is another attractive thing about essay writing. I interact with people all over the globe, in all time zones, all with immediacy, just like I am there. The whole time, the people I work with think I am somewhere near them. The mystery and intrigue of these situations always makes me smile, and the code number that replaces my name adds to the secret agent feel of my position. I am Jeffrey Alfred Ruth, a.k.a. Ossi Chesterton, a.k.a. Writer 76197, a.k.a. The Ghostwriter. You, the client, will never hear my voice, will never see my face, and your order will appear instantly on your screen, at which point you will never hear from me again. By the time that you are reviewing your paper for errors that simply do not exist, I will be enjoying a martini at the bar and grill. Oh yes, the martini will be shaken, not stirred, and will always have blue cheese stuffed olives. Have a nice night.

As I expected at the outset of this Shakespeare order, the problems are growing exponentially. To keep score, I review all the things that are wrong about this situation. Not only does the parent know that her son is cheating on his school work, she is helping him do so. Not only is she helping him, but she is acting as advocate/secretary for the matter. To make matters worse, they are Australian, which means that I have to adjust the language of the paper itself. I'll have to remember to submit a reimbursable expense charge to Tonya for this, since Australian English isn't my norm. There's more to this sort of writing than simply adding a few *walkabouts, mates,* and other jargon to the essay. This will take some skill, precision, and forethought before I declare the assignment ready to submit. I am somewhat disappointed and surprised at this complication. Usually, the order itself will indicate that the paper requires a U.K. or Australian writer. If I don't feel like writing as the Queen of England, or Quigley Down Under, then I can simply discard the order. Oh well, I'm committed this time, for better or worse.

I can't help but laugh at what seems to me to be maternal instinct on the part of the Aussie client. She had written, "His professor will be mad if [her son] is e-mailing in class." So, his mom didn't want her precious baby in trouble during class! That is really touching. I wonder what she would think if her son was caught turning in a paper from an essay writing service? Wouldn't that be a bigger issue? In a way, I can take that as a compliment, I suppose. If the parent is so concerned about problems with the instructor, and if she still uses my service, then she must not be concerned that I will cause problems. Again, that is really touching. I will make sure that there are no more problems than already noted. Now that I have the coffee/martini conundrum decided, it is time to approach the work, solve for the current issue, and earn the money.

I would have to assume that the client's urgency in getting his mom to talk with me must be regarding the subject or topic of the paper. After all, the simple request for a paper about, "Romance and Tragedy in William Shakespeare's *Romeo and Juliet,*" is more than a bit vague. I hope that he has something just a little more specific in mind. As any scholar knows, and anyone who has ever hired a scholar should know, a research paper must have a provable, supportable thesis, not just an idea. Mom wasn't exactly illuminating me on this, and I don't have time to waste. Double clicking the order on the screen brings up two important things: the details and supporting information of the order, and more importantly, the Clock. Yes, this gets a capital "C." It is what rules the forger's world.

The adage "Time is Money" must have been coined by a forger.

This saying is true in both positive and negative manner. Time is money because shorter deadlines get charged more to the clients. They must pay for speedy delivery. On the contrary, time is money can also be constructed to mean waste of time is waste of money. To the forger, missing a deadline, i.e., not paying attention to the Clock, means a substantial financial penalty. Time and money are forever intertwined, and absolutely govern the life and lifestyle of the academic forger. When I joined Fraud-Papers, the employment manual described the process by which a writer can request a deadline extension, but also made it abundantly clear that this should never, ever, be done. The company does not want clients to be disappointed in any fashion, because there are too many other companies out there providing this service. A disappointed customer will become a newly appointed customer elsewhere.

With this in mind, I look at the Clock for order 179934. There are only six hours left. That sure explains the phone call. They must be going crazy, thinking about writing a four to six page Shakespeare paper by then. It occurs to me again that they don't even have a specific plan in mind as to what to write. Knowing that I can't talk to protective mum, and the actual client is not available, I decide to just pick an approach based upon my personal knowledge and expertise, and make sure everything just follows the instructions provided when they placed the order. If I get this all right, and pay strict attention to the Clock, then all will be well. To be more specific, the paper will be "Just so." I smile and start typing.

I spend the next couple of hours (two hours and seven minutes, to be exact, according to the Clock) postulating that there is no difference between romance and tragedy in this play, because romance and tragedy are in fact the same thing. The loving gestures of the characters are simultaneously gestures that kill their lovers. There is usually some sense of irony that I enjoy while working for clients, something that I plant in the paper and then watch blossom. In this case, I figure that my loving gesture of writing a quality paper for this client will kill the client either by lightening his wallet, or by his instructor finding out and killing him … or his mum killing him, I suppose. I hope this is all metaphoric, and doesn't find its way into tomorrow's headlines in any time zone. In any event, I have everything wrapped up with plenty of time left. A couple deft and time-honed clicks on the computer screen places the completed order into the client's hands, again, metaphorically speaking.

Now it's time for the finishing touches. As with the previous e-mail exchanges with Mom Client, I have a special template that I use, and can type in a few seconds, perfectly from memory. "Dear Client, I have completed your order and sent it to you. It should be available momentarily. The paper follows your instructions exactly, and is formatted to the current standards. If you have any questions or concerns, please message me and I will respond immediately. Please remember to complete and submit a survey to the company. Thank you again for your order, Writer 76197." Now isn't that nice? It usually results in the client not having any questions, being convinced by the message that all is well, as I mentioned before, and filling out a positive survey which will ultimately benefit me. This is especially true when an order is completed well before the deadline, which also goes a long way to satisfying customers. Again, time is money.

Time to knock off for the night. I always try to finish a session with a particularly satisfying order, especially one that has a bit of humor, or should I write, *humour*, to it. What started off as a typical Shakespeare order turned out to have just the quirky ups, downs, and twists that I enjoy so much. I'll take the happy feelings out for a brisk, evening walk. Just before I shut off the computer, it chimes at me one last time. Do I dare take a look? I really can't help myself.

It's Aussie mum again, with a final message. "Dear Writer 76197, my son just got in from school as we got the paper. Lovely! Who'd have known that love and a good killing can be such bedmates? Good on you! A favorable survey's on its way straight to the company for you. Cheers, then."

What a great ending to this evening. Think I'll take that martini after all, out on the boardwalk with me. I'm quite the happy forger tonight. Good on me!—Ossi.

2. Sometime in 2011, I was approached by a client who was looking to advance his academic career through the use of scholarship funding. This is an admirable effort, and shows a certain level of motivation, as well. Well, perhaps not a great deal of motivation, unless one considers hiring a forger to do the work to fall under this category.

To gain this particular scholarship, i.e., to win the contest, applicants had to write a three-to five-point plan to educate newly-elected members of the 112th Congress of the United States. It seems that this national membership organization who had structured the competition was urging students entering master's degree programs to participate in making sure that these legislative freshmen were aware of critical issues of both population growth and illegal immigration.

Submissions were to be between 500 and 750 words, written in English, word-processed or typed double-spaced using one side of 8.5" × 11" white paper, in Times Roman or Arial size 12–14 font. That is, ironically, typical of general forgers' orders. What is not so common is a customer using a forger to win a scholarship. No ethical dilemma there, right? This student was in direct competition not with his own grades, but with peers attempting to get into a graduate degree program. Not only is he cheating his own integrity, but he is cheating any other well-deserving student who is honest. It is stealing from everyone.

3. Speaking of ethics, this one is quite special, as well. It was certainly memorable and provided a good laugh. The order indicated that it was for an exam. The test included 20 essay questions that had to be answered thoroughly. That sounded basic enough. Here's the twist: the subject matter was the profession of ethics.

Yes, ethics.

The instructions from the faculty leading this course did mention to the students that there was an important caveat, which of course was forwarded to the potential academic forger. It stated that for some of the questions, there would be more than one ethical guideline that pertained to the scenario, and which would have to be explored to gain full credit. Presumably, the ethical guidelines of the cheating student and the academic forger would not qualify for more than one ethical guideline or point of view.

Further, the order stated that it was not an open book exam, so there were to be no text or other sources to be consulted. And the kicker? Warning: this exam will be submitted to a plagiarism detection site, so it must be original. Of course it would be original! It would be the academic forger's original work. That qualifies. Fortunately, the customer did let the forger know about this "problem." It was provided before the order comments that gave the student's username and password. Yes, he gave identifying information which could later be traced, but to get into the test, he really had to. The final instruction really made my day:

Dear Writer, please remember to click on the "academic honesty" box.

Which One Is the Forgery? A Four Paper Challenge

Here, then, is a fun exercise for educators, not to mention interested students and their parents. Four short academic papers follow. There are two on Voltaire's *Candide*, and two which cover Charlotte Perkins Gilman's "The Yellow Wallpaper." These are two papers commonly assigned during the freshman year of a standard American baccalaureate program. Nearly every undergrad will come across at least one of these, whether he is an English major or not.

Needless to say, they also represent simple forgers' fodder.

Which paper is the forgery, and which ones are actual students' work? Read on. After the fourth essay, the answer will be revealed.

Candide: Situational and Global Satire

What makes Voltaire's *Candide* such an intriguing work is its use of satire. By raising subjects and then ironically placing, treating, or ridiculing that theme, he creates within the reader a series of new thought patterns and interpretations. The result is a piece of literature that is multilayered and efficient at expressing itself.

There are three points that stand out in Voltaire's use of satire. The first is the initial description of characters and their traits, which are then refuted by book's end. In this way, Voltaire creates a social satire. He points out not only the foibles of a judgmental society, but also cleverly brings into question the reader's own biases. This occurs with the appearance of Candide early in the book. Though living in the castle of a baron he is presented as an innocent buffoon. He is taken advantage of by Miss Cunegonde as she desires experimental passion (Voltaire 16), and he believes in everything that the insincere Pangloss states. As a result readers receive what they expect from this less-than-inspiring main character. He is banished from the castle, and then taken advantage of all over again in the Bulgars' camp. Once he has run the gauntlet it appears that the case is settled. Candide is only a naïve child-man. But that is where the stage is perfectly set for this sort of satire. The same innocence that makes Candide believe his free will can preserve him ultimately does. He redeems himself in growing fashion until finally the reader understands that he is actually not the low-intellect simpleton, but the strong hearted protagonist of the novel.

A simpler expression is found in the vignette of the admiral's court-martial (Voltaire 48). Candide and Martin happen upon this alleged spy who is about to be executed for failing to properly wage war. This possesses the ring of serious tone to it. One would expect a harsh observation either of war in general or the traits of the military machine. However this is not to be. As Candide observes, the execution proceeds, but with an interesting caveat. It appears that the punishment is meant to "encourage the others to fight" (49). Voltaire is clearly satirizing the notion of the military's moral values and perhaps even the appropriate place of war in modern society.

These examples both work together to support the more global theme of the destruction of futilistic optimism. This view on the optimistic outlook begins with an original sense of futility (hence the name). As seen above Candide does possess a naturally favorable, if somewhat unrefined, view of life. He imagines that if he just keeps trying to please people and choose basic right over wrong, acquiescence over quarrel, that he will prevail and enjoy the benefits of living. By the second chapter Voltaire's novel declares this optimism to be quite futile. Candide is banished and beaten. The enforcement of law in the military is a farce. Pangloss's assertion that this is what happens when one believes too strongly in the best of things seems to confirm this. Author Dawn Sova in *Literature Suppressed on Sexual Grounds* offers this assessment. "*Candide* is a satire of optimism and of the belief 'that the world is the best of all possible worlds and everything in it is a necessary evil'" (34). Sova has a point—this world of Voltaire's challenges the notion that everything in it is the best of all things. However the philosophy of futilistic optimism is itself destroyed in the end. Candide the character and *Candide* the book end well and satisfy those readers inclined to sympathy. In Candide's inner happiness is the confirmation that the things that are bad about the world just aren't as bad as they seem.

Satire is what *Candide* is all about. From the general perspective of the novel as satire to the individualized portrayals of characters and incidents it is clear: the book is intended to be read on two levels— enjoyable description and social commentary.

References

Sova, Dawn. *Literature Suppressed on Sexual Grounds*. New York: InfoBase, 2006. Print.

Voltaire. *Candide and Other Stories*. New York: Simon & Schuster, 2005. Print.

Voltaire's *Candide*: Contemporary Criticism

Voltaire's *Candide*, in addition to its literary merit, is even more important as a historical document. Its pages and its storyline offer a running commentary on the Europe that he, and other intellectuals, lived in. As perhaps can be assumed, books of this nature can be quite critical of the powers-that-be. This is certainly true of *Candide*.

In the case of *Candide*, there are two main considerations to be undertaken when reading. The first one that springs from the pages is the overarching criticism of the government of the modern state, and also the Roman Catholic Church. A close reading of the chapters describing the Old Man of Eldorado reveals this well. The Roman Catholic church of Voltaire's time was stifling. It maintained that religion was not a personal experience. That is to say, that a man could not, and did not, directly approach God. He had to come to the Roman Catholic Church, and its priests, to experience God and his blessings (or condemnations, as the case may be). Due to this, there was an inordinate amount of power vested in these near demi–Gods called priests. They maintained a hierarchy that started with the local pastor, and extended up through the bishops, cardinals, and eventually to the Pope himself in Rome.

Voltaire fought this setup in his writing, and especially in *Candide*. To look into Chapter Eighteen, it doesn't take much reading between the lines to experience this satire.

The Old Man is described right off as being, "...the most learned man in the whole country," and this is immediately contrasted with the citizenry of the land which were "ignorant and comfortable" in their lives (60). That is quite a historical statement that Voltaire is making. He is directly placing what the intellectual observes against the nominal way of life for the typical citizenry. And what, historically, is he trying to say about this comfortable ignorance? The Old Man is the answer here. When asked about why his town's view of religion works so well compared to the surrounding areas, the exchange goes like this: "You have no monks to teach, to argue, to govern, and to plot and to burn alive those who don't share their views?" "We'd have to be out of our minds [if we did]" is his answer (62).

This conversation, and the chapter in which it takes place, offers biting historical context. First of all, Voltaire is describing the far-too-reaching powers of the church at the time. The Roman Catholic priests simply weren't there to assist parishioners in their search for salvation. In fact, the close reader finds that of all the things in the list above, salvation and care are not even mentioned. Rather, what are mentioned are the problems of the church for real people of Europe during the Enlightenment, period. Instead of being a calming, loving, instrument of salvation and God's blessing, the church had taken to persecuting the growing intellectualism and humanism that was being produced. So instead of love and blessing, the list above degrades down to arguing, plotting and burning. All of these actions were taken by the historical Roman Catholic Church. They did indeed attempt to thwart the new science that was emerging during this period. They did go after those who would attempt to put the traditional views of an Earth centered Universe on trial. In Voltaire's *Candide*, the experience of the Old Man and Eldorado, with their hands-off religion, is a much better alternative. It is a message to the Roman Catholic Church of the Enlightenment Period.

It is not just the Roman Catholic Church that Voltaire attacks in his writing. The government also comes under fire. The most striking of these satirical observations comes through the concept and topic of warfare as visited by the government. This represents the abuse of power that was commonly associated with the state, and ties in to the frequent wars of the period. His satire is quite clear. As Candide, the character, runs through villages in the early part of the novel, he encounters the horror of war, which he remarks as being quite normal and in accordance with international laws (8). What is the result of following the natural rights and laws of the state? Beaten old men, slaughtered women, and raped and disemboweled girls, to name a few. These passages clearly represent the intellectuals' Enlightenment rebuttal of the growing, and abusive, powers of the state.

The context that informs *Candide* holds the key to understanding where Voltaire's ideas for the work came from. Overall, the Enlighten-ment Period itself is the thrust of what is found in the novel. This time, occurring mainly in the very middle of the 1700s across all of Western Europe, was possessed with a class of men who began to take independ-ence and liberty from the establishments around them. They deemed it necessary, for perhaps the first time, to challenge the accepted ignorance of men who relied on the Church and the state to do the thinking for them. Therefore intellectuals and philosophers such as Voltaire began to seed their writing with this progressive thinking. Several key moments had already taken place by the writing of *Candide* that must be found as influencing his positions. These include the events at the end of the century prior to his publications, and which set forth the traditional boundary of the beginning of the Enlightenment. The Thirty-Years War, the persecution of Isaac Newton, and likewise the persecution of Galileo are chief among these, as they represent the state, and Church, attempts to crush intellectual ambitions of the thinkers. It is easy to assume, also, that the Protestant Reformation of the early Enlightenment could have been the catalyst for the chapter on the Old Man and Eldorado.

Overall, then, *Candide* by Voltaire operates less like a novel, and more like a historical criticism. Based on its satirical themes, and the contemporary and past events of Europe surrounding this writing, a close reading can reveal nothing else quite so clearly.

References

Voltaire. *Candide.* New Haven, CT: Yale University Press, 2005. Print.

Irony and Metaphor:
The Powers Behind "The Yellow Wallpaper"

Charlotte Perkins Gilman's "The Yellow Wallpaper" is a short story that is not to be believed. What is meant by that is the language is profoundly ironic, and metaphoric. There is not much that can be taken quite literally. Three particular forms of this language are found in the text. First is the use of verbal irony on the part of the narrator. Second is the use of symbolic irony. Consistent metaphors make up the final element of this clever use of language. All three of these concepts together make up the mysterious verbiage of the short, but effective tale.

Verbal irony deserves the most credit in the complex web of symbolic language that Gilman uses. Especially since the story depends, even revolves completely around, the narrator's voice, her choice of words makes up the bulk of the meaning of the action. With such pervasive use of a narrative element, it is beneficial to analyze the overall paper with a look, chronologically, at how the language is used. The very first sentence begins to allow some sense of the paradox that irony brings to the story, and why it is so easily found. The words, "mere ordinary people like John and myself" next to the words "ancestral hall" (537), automatically place the beginning of the sentence and the second sense at odds, realistically speaking. It is not just "seldom" that this occurs. The odds are much slimmer than that. This automatically puts the reader on alert that all may not be as the narrator claims. An element of doubt begins to creep in. Again, the voice of the narrator intrudes upon normalcy lines later. "Still I will proudly declare that there is something queer about it," she relates. Now that is queer all by itself. Her tone is verbally ironic, because there is no reason for her to be proud about this declaration. Unless, she is on the defensive. Her words become ironic, as she is not being proud, but protecting herself. The question becomes, protecting herself from what? Perhaps it is from her own husband. He surely is the target of the next placement of verbal irony. She describes him as practical (537). However he is not merely practical, but practical "in the extreme." Again, the juxtaposition of these two words is plainly ironic. Practical is such a conservative rendering of a character trait, that to treat it as anything approaching radical is beyond the pale. It places the statement into the cynical realm, and again makes the reader question the narrator. The mistrust grows with each demonstration of verbal irony instead of verbal realism. By the beginning of the second page of the story, Gilman's narrator has lost even more touch with both reality, and the reader's trust level. And again, the irony is based upon the practical John. It has already been established by this point that he is practical, and one can expect him to be practical and not wild in his judgments, then, as well. Even more so, he is identified by his wife as being "a physician of high standing" in addition to being her husband (538). This should necessarily indicate just how trustworthy he is, and how the narrator is reliant upon him. But that turns out not to be the case at all. She openly questions him with, "You see he does not believe I am sick!" This is not what one would expect from the woman at all. What is much more anticipated, if she were sick, would be her physician/husband's description of her malady, not his derision. In the space of a mere page or so, Charlotte Perkins Gilman has managed to use verbal irony to turn reality upon its end for the reader to enjoy.

Symbolic irony liberally spread through the story also increases the suspension of reality and assists the reader in his efforts to see through what the narrator is saying. Perhaps the first example of this is the placement of the physician into the story (538). One would expect, again, that this would indicate a rational sort of tale. It would be under the guidance, the supervision perhaps, of this character. Nothing too out of the ordinary regarding illness or disease should occur. Yet that is exactly what will happen, as the reader discovers. To ensure that this important ironic point is not missed, it is revealed that the narrator's brother is also a physician. Repetition often indicates to readers that the point is quite important. Certainly the symbolic irony of "physician" is one of those important points. The setting itself becomes symbolic irony as well, as it is described as a "beautiful place" (538). As the story moves along, this beautiful place is quite the opposite for the main character. It ends up driving her literally quite mad, and she does not find comfort in it at all, as would be expected by the description of this symbol, the house. Once the mansion is described, and the woman begins to describe her room, again one finds a symbol of irony. It is the yellow color itself. Yellow is normally associated with happy things and happy moments.

It is also one of the less oppressive colors one may have in a room. In fact, the room is, at least temporarily, described by the woman as being, "a big, airy room" (539). So how does the description manage to change so quickly when the innocuous color is being considered? It is because this nominal shade is being used as a symbol of irony. It is yet another clue that the location it is found in, the woman's room, holds further clue to the deepening mystery of "The Yellow Wallpaper." It is while in the room that the woman reveals another ironic symbol that Gilman utilizes. It is the writing of the narrator. It is at once two completely separate things. At first, it is a fine undertaking that the woman should do to calm herself and enjoy as a creative outlet. Her husband recommends her to this, that she, "ought to use [her] will and good sense to check the tendency" (540). That seems urbane enough. Yet on the next page, the woman who is writing treats this as something forbidden (541). "I must not let her find me writing," she frets (541). If the writing was recommended to her and her husband knew about it and encouraged it, then why would it at the same time be taboo? Why does the narrator have to worry to such an extent about the activity? It is because the writing is symbolic irony for all of the rest of the strange twists upon reality that are going on.

Consistent uses of metaphors through "The Yellow Wallpaper" continue to remind the reader of the anticipation of a negative end that must await the narrator. There is no reprieve from the incidence of these reminders. A reader could almost point to any paragraph and find these warning signs. Many of them directly concern the relationship of the woman to the wallpaper itself, as the story moves to its inevitable end of madness. What does she first describe the paper as having—even as she first beholds it? It has a spot where, "the pattern lolls like a broken neck" and that it also possesses, "bulbous eyes" (540). This is hardly what one would expect when describing room décor. The paper, in this fashion, must be used as a metaphor. Finally, reality is reflected, and it doesn't look healthy. Then there is the floor. What kind of a floor is it? Not smooth, and inviting. It has scratches and gouges and splinters (541). What could this represent metaphorically? It sounds as if this is increasingly connected with the narrator's state of mind. It is becoming worn, and not well-worn, but tormented. As she rapidly retreats into her own mind, she talks of the bed that she is being forced to sleep in. This "immovable bed" (542) is a metaphor of upcoming death, either of mind or body, of the woman. This is apparent, as she talks of it as one would describe a coffin. It is not able to be moved, one lies on it (or in it, figuratively), and it is nailed to the floor, she believes. It is interestingly that she mentions nails, as the common understanding of nails used in this manner can be that of nails in a coffin. It all fits, and the bed quickly becomes a metaphor of the kind of ending one is increasingly able to predict. Things are all adding up. Finally, two more metaphors veritably sneak into the narrative regarding the room, and the wallpaper. Together, they are hard to deny in their impact. The first is the specific naming of the room by the woman as a "nursery" (543). Though she had alluded to the fact that children must have spent time in the room, as she earlier blames these figures for the damage to the wallpaper and other things, she had never specifically called the chamber anything else but a room. Now it becomes a nursery all of a sudden. This is metaphorical of the state of the woman. She is retreating away from the world of adulthood. She is literally shrinking away before the reader's very eyes. It is also metaphoric of a lack of responsibility that the woman now has in her diminished state. The second of these metaphors is the description of the woman inside the pattern of the wallpaper. The narrator is beginning to admit to the reader that she is being transformed into this vision; this despite the fact that it may not be a conscious admission. The woman on the wall is "stooping and creeping about behind the pattern," and the narrator doesn't like it at all (543). Is this because it represents herself and the unusual, and perhaps even sinister, behavior that she is personally expressing? Is it maybe a moment of clarity on the part of the woman who is losing her grip on reality? There can be no argument rationally made for why else the figure on the wallpaper would be a woman. She is seeing herself, almost as if the wallpaper were a metaphorical mirror. Eventually, the wallpaper itself grows beyond its own faded reality and becomes the ultimate metaphor for the lady's mind. As she sits, or lies, on the bed, day after day she has time to ponder the degradation of the pattern before her. It has, "a lack of sequence, a defiance of law," and is a "constant irritant to a normal mind" (544). The pattern has now become an instrument of torture to her, not only an irritant, indicating that her mind is, in fact, not the normal mind she was just referring to. As her mind decays, the reader is instructed of the progress. The toadstools, the fungus she sees in the wallpaper grow new shoots daily, and other "foul, bad yellow things" grow with these shoots (545). The smell of decay is one of the last metaphors that presage the final end. One needs very little instruction to perceive the metaphor of death—again, of mind or body. The series of metaphors has worked.

Charlotte Perkins Gilman crafts a thorough development of madness in "The Yellow Wallpaper." Through use of verbal and symbolic irony, along with a lengthy and progressive series of metaphors, the reader is encouraged to follow the narrator down a long, mysterious journey to her mental end.

References

Gilman, Charlotte Perkins. "The Yellow Wallpaper." *The Norton Introduction to Literature Shorter Eighth Edition*. Eds. Jerome Beaty, Alison Booth, J. Paul Hunter, and Kelly J. Mays. New York: W.W. Norton, 2002. 537–549.

Subtle Symbols: The Powers Behind "The Yellow Wallpaper"

The short story "The Yellow Wallpaper," by Charlotte Perkins Gilman, is a fine example of the successful use of symbolism to create a tone in literature. The success comes not only from the fact that symbols are used, which is commonplace among fiction. It comes from the fact that many symbols used are hidden and subtle. That is because the symbols are woven into the story as background to the action itself, and can nearly be missed as the reading proceeds and the story unfolds. It is only at the close of the action that the powerful workings of the symbolism make it clear that it is the tone that is more important than the action itself in working out the meaning to this clever and harrowing tale of the descent into madness.

The first of the hidden symbols should be quite explicit in nature, but again it is introduced in such a mundane sense that it is not evident at first. This symbol is the fact that the narrator's husband is a doctor. Not only is he a doctor but he is in fact a doctor of renown and this detail holds the importance. The husband is introduced as, "a physician of high standing" (1). The reason that this symbol is of primary importance is that it sets the tone of narrator against everyone else—including against reality. The mention by the protagonist of the fact that she feels that the doctor, her own husband, is against her, forces one to immediately make one of two choices. First, the reader may choose to believe the first, obvious layer. That is to say, that the narrator is trustworthy. This would be the clear first choice because the narrator has pitted herself against the other characters, and as she is telling the story the reader could easily be swayed in her direction. However, the second choice that could be made is that the narrator is not in her right mind, and that by contending with the doctor of high renown, and her own husband, she is lying or delusional, thereby influencing the reading of "The Yellow Wallpaper." By story's end, it is clear that the description of the physician is a hidden symbol, tucked under the first layer of reading. It represents the fight against reality that the poor woman's mind is going through.

It is not enough to merely make the statement that another important symbol in "The Yellow Wallpaper" is the paper itself. That is too plain and obvious. One must point to a specific instance or mention of the wallpaper for it to have genuine symbolism. The symbol that most stands out after a close reading is one of the first descriptions the woman offers. She describes the wallpaper's pattern as having eyes (3). At first they are "bulbous eyes [which] stare at you." Moments later they are "absurd, unblinking eyes." The eyes in the pattern of the paper do not exist. Clearly they are manifestations of the woman's paranoia, and it is in that observation that they hold symbolic value. The narrator has a fear, both reasonable and unreasonable, of being observed at all times. This symbol then of the ever-watching eyes shows that. She is actually being guardedly observed around the clock by both the physician/ husband, and by his sister (more on those two later), and she resents it. That is the reality which the symbol points to. However, there is also the irrational side that the symbol points to, as well. It is not enough that the woman disdains the actual watching over that she receives. It has spread into her feeling that she is being watched at all times now, even when people aren't actually there to do so. The wallpaper with its symbolic eyes demonstrates this irrational fear and resentment.

A third symbol—or perhaps pair of symbols would be more accurate—is that of the husband and his sister. Who are these people? Are they really who the narrator claims, or are they actually symbols that represent something else? This is one of the most discussed and intriguing aspects of "The Yellow Wallpaper." If one is to doubt the sincerity and truth of certain things that the narrator describes, then why believe anything that she states? Clearly everything must be held up and carefully observed that she presents. Once the woman's mental stability comes into question, the reader is absolutely obligated to consider the truth of even the basic facts of the story. Is it truly likely that the physician and the sister are actually who she says they are? No. In fact, it is highly unlikely. The reader only needs to look at the actual roles that these characters play in order to determine the truth. Before it is even let out that John and she are married, the woman states that, "John laughs at me…" (1). This is an interesting comment to begin her description of her husband. She spends much more time discussing his scientific and psychological beliefs and observations and how much he "scoffs openly." In fact, this is the pattern found in John. He laughs at her and mocks her. If he truly were her husband, he is a poor showing of one. This leads the reader to consider, then, John's alleged sister. She comes into the story only by the fourth page. One would expect that if she had moved in with the woman and her husband that she would have been mentioned much earlier. Again, the hidden symbolism is in her role. She is there only to come up and spy on her (4). She is not John's sister—she is working with him. It is not too much to figure this whole thing out by story's end. John is indeed a physician. He is a psychiatrist of renown that is in charge of the woman's case. The sister that the woman complains about is not John's sister, but is in fact Doctor John's nurse. Therefore the titles of husband and sister are mere symbols that do not reflect reality. They are symbols that reflect the misgivings of a woman who believes that she is being abandoned by the world and she represents this by showing that even family members regard her with clinical attachment, even when they are not truly family members at all.

There are many symbols in Gilman's "The Yellow Wallpaper." Though many are obvious, the more subtle ones such as the use of the doctor, the relationship of husband and his sister, and the eyes of the wallpaper, offer the most compelling and fascinating elements to the understanding of the thrust of the story itself.

References

Gilman, Charlotte Perkins. "The Yellow Wallpaper." *Literature: An Introduction to Reading and Writing*. 10th ed. Eds. Edgar V. Roberts, and Robert Zweig. New York: Pearson, 2011. 537–549. Print.

> Here, then, is the answer. As many of you might have guessed by now, these very middle-of-the-road papers are forgettable and would not stand out on any professor's desk across America.
>
> That is because all four are the products of an academic forger.

Chapter Notes

Preface

1. S. F. Davis, T. B. Gallant, and P. F. Drinan (2009). *Cheating in School: What We Know and What We Can Do*. Malden, MA: Wiley-Blackwell.

2. D.L. McCabe, K.D. Butterfield, and L.K. Treviño (2012). *Cheating in College: Why Students do It and What Educators can do About It*. Baltimore: The Johns Hopkins University Press.

3. D. Tomar (2013). *The Shadow Scholar: How I Made a Living Helping College Kids Cheat*. New York: Bloomsbury.

Chapter 5

1. This is an actual, very typical web search that students seeking to buy an essay would encounter. Although I offer this result without identifying the company at the end of it, I would encourage those interested in the particulars to try this several times, choosing different services each time to compare findings.

Chapter 7

1. These are very conservative numbers. As a senior staff writer, my home page with FraudPapers provided the latest statistics, updated hourly, regarding numbers of writers, numbers of active writers on that specific day, numbers of orders taken, completed, submitted, and numerous other figures. I have intentionally rounded down somewhat, in an effort to not overstate the field of academic forgery. That being said, the overall numbers remain staggering.

2. U.S. Department of Education, National Center for Education Statistics (2013). *Digest of Education Statistics, 2012* (NCES 2014–015), Table 5.

Chapter 9

1. For a related story of this sort of fraud, see Tony Patterson's 2 March 2011 article for *The Independent*: "German Defence Minister Quits Over PhD Plagiarism Scandal." *The Independent*. Retrieved from http://www.independent.co.uk/news/world/

europe/german-defence-minister-quits-over-phd-plagiarism-scandal-2229492.
html

Chapter 14

1. U.S. Copyright Office. (2014). *Complete Version of the U.S. Copyright Law, December 2011*. Retrieved from http://www.copyright.gov/title17/

Chapter 15

1. Massachusetts Institute of Technology (2014). *Resources for Teachers: How to Detect Plagiarism*. Retrieved from http://writing.mit.edu/wcc/resources/teachers/detectplagiarism
2. R. Pérez-Peña (7 September 2012). Studies Find More Students Cheating, With High Achievers no Exception. *The New York Times*. Retrieved from http://www.nytimes.com/2012/09/08/education/studies-show-more-students-cheat-even-high-achievers.html?emc=eta1&_r=1&
3. For an easily searchable link to New York's state laws covering this subject, see YPDCrime.com: YPDCrime.com. (2014). *Article 170—NY Penal Law*. Retrieved from http://ypdcrime.com/penal.law/article170.htm#p170.10

References

Davis, S. F., T. B. Gallant, and P. F. Drinan. 2009. *Cheating in School: What We Know and What We Can Do.* Malden, MA: Wiley-Blackwell.

Massachusetts Institute of Technology. 2014. *Resources for Teachers: How to Detect Plagiarism.* Retrieved from http://writing.mit.edu/wcc/resources/tea chers/detectplagiarism

McCabe, D.L., K.D. Butterfield, and L.K. Treviño. 2012. *Cheating in College: Why Students Do It and What Educators Can Do About It.* Baltimore: The Johns Hopkins University Press.

Patterson, T. 2011. "German Defence Minister Quits Over PhD Plagiarism Scandal." *The Independent.* Retrieved from http://www.independent.co.uk/news/ world/europe/german-defence-minister-quits-over-phd-plagiarism-scandal-2229492.html

Pérez-Peña, R. 7 September 2012. "Studies Find More Students Cheating, With High Achievers No Exception." *The New York Times.* Retrieved from http:// www.nytimes.com/2012/09/08/education/studies-show-more-students-cheat-even-high-achievers.html?emc=eta1&_r=1&

Tomar, D. 2013. *The Shadow Scholar: How I Made a Living Helping College Kids Cheat.* New York: Bloomsbury.

U.S. Copyright Office. 2014. *Complete Version of the U.S. Copyright Law, December 2011.* Retrieved from http://www.copyright.gov/title17/

U.S. Department of Education, National Center for Education Statistics. 2013. *Digest of Education Statistics, 2012* (NCES 2014–015), Table 5.

YPDCrime.com. 2014. *Article 170—NY Penal Law.* Retrieved from http://ypd crime.com/penal.law/article170.htm#p170.10

Index